Anatomy of
Nonfiction

Writing True Stories for Children

Margery Facklam and Peggy Thomas

Writer's Institute
Publications

www.WritersInstitutePublications.com

About the Authors

Margery Facklam has written more than 40 nonfiction books for children and young adults including *The Big Bug Book*, *Only a Star*, and *Bees Dance and Whales Sing*. Many of her books have been named NSTA-CBC Outstanding Science Trade Books, New York Public Library Books for the Teen Age, American Booksellers Association Pick of the Lists, and ALA Notable Books. In 2005, she was honored with the New York State Library Association's Knickerbocker Award, for excellence in her body of work as a New York State author. Margery was a longtime instructor for the Institute of Children's Literature, and also previously served as Director of Education at the Buffalo Museum of Science, Niagara Falls Aquarium, and the Buffalo Zoo.

Peggy Thomas is the author of more than 17 books for children and young adults, among them the award-winning *Farmer George Plants a Nation*, named an Outstanding Science Trade Book, a *School Library Journal* Best Book, and Best Children's Book by the Farm Bureaus of Ohio, Wisconsin, and Nebraska. Her books have frequently been designated Outstanding Science Trade Books, New York Public Library Books for the Teen Age, and ALA Recommended Books for Reluctant Young Adult Readers. Peggy is an instructor for the Institute of Children's Literature and a frequent speaker at schools and writing conferences.

Editors

Pamela Glass Kelly
Meredith DeSousa

Design and Production Editor

Joanna Horvath

Illustrations supplied by iStockphoto and Dreamstime.

International Standard Book Number 978-1-889715-59-9

1-800-443-6078. www.WritersBookstore.com
E-mail: Services@WritersBookstore.com

Printed and bound in Canada.

To Barbara Lucas, an extraordinary editor and even better friend. —*MF*

To Mom, with love. Thanks for teaching me all you know. —*PT*

Write what should not be forgotten. —Isabel Allende

Acknowledgments

This book would have been much slimmer without all the writers who graciously shared their experiences, weighed in on certain issues, and of course created excellent nonfiction that we could then share with you. Thank you to Ann Bausum, Karen Beil, Fred Bortz, Roxanne Chadwick, Jan Fields, Jim Giblin, Richard and Janet Graber, Barbara Kerley, Mary Bowman Kruhm, Hope Marston, Joanne Mattern, Carla McClafferty, Mary Meinking, Jim Murphy, Cathy Nanz, Q. L. Pearce, Dana Rau, Mary Scarbrough, Steve Swinburne, Trudi Trueit, Nancy Whitelaw, and Bill Zinsser.

We picked the brains of editors too, especially Adrienne Mason, Chandra Howard, John Riley, David Dilkes, Ben Rosenthal, Stephen Roxburgh, and Hillary Breed Van Dusen. Editors Randi Rivers and Carolyn Yoder were bothered more than once, and we owe a special debt of gratitude to Barbara Lucas, who taught us both about the business. We also appreciate the professional help from librarians, especially Marie Bindeman, Director of the Lockport Library, and Suzanne Shearman at Barclay Elementary, for their insight.

To all our students who shared their writing journeys with us, thank you. We probably learned more from you than you learned from us. And thanks to all of our critique buddies over the years including Mary Ryan, Sallie Randolph, Alice DeLa Croix, Carol Johmann, Judy Bradbury, Jan Czech, Sibby Falk, Kathy Blasi, and especially M. J. Auch for many years of laughter and great stories. If we have overlooked anyone, we apologize and thank you too.

Table of Contents

Introduction

Writing in the Blood

"Satisfaction of one's curiosity is one of the greatest
sources of happiness in life."

—Linus Pauling

No two writers work precisely the same way—not even mother and
daughter. We share many of the same views on writing nonfiction, and
our processes are similar, but our experiences in the publishing industry, which
span more than 50 years, have been different. In 1960, I typed my first book,
Whistle For Danger, on a Smith-Corona typewriter using onionskin and carbon
paper. Thirty years later, Peggy wrote her first book, *Volcano*, using one of the
first state-of-the-art word processors—a Kaypro that opened like a breadbox—
using 5-inch floppy disks. But more has changed than technology. The business
of children's publishing has changed, education has changed, and children
have changed.

This book is a collaboration of two authors and the sum of what we have
learned in the process of researching and writing more than 50 books of
nonfiction. Dissecting nonfiction as we have made us look at what we do in a
different light. We sought out second opinions and received the generous help
of experts and specialists in their fields. As a result we learned things we hadn't
thought about before, and became even more inspired by the limitless potential of our nonfiction craft to touch children's lives. We hope that, after reading
this book, you'll begin your own writing journey with a similar inspiration—
and a motivation to make your mark in a world of true stories.

Margery's Story: It All Started with Snakes

I was the kind of kid who kept a snake in my bedroom until my sister objected, and I spent almost every Saturday at the Buffalo Museum of Science. In those days, kids could go there without adults and take the most amazing classes—everything from astronomy to zoology. By the time I was in high school, I had become fascinated by herpetology, the study of reptiles. When I outgrew the museum, I volunteered at the Buffalo Zoo, where I cleaned cages and fed snakes because most of the regular keepers were fighting in World War II.

I earned my tuition at the University of Buffalo by cleaning cages in the biology department's animal house. The professor I worked with studied porcupines, so I quickly learned how to wash a porcupine, and even carried the first baby "porcupet" to classes with me to feed it with a doll's bottle.

By the time I graduated, the war had ended, and I had the good fortune to fall in love with and eventually marry Howard Facklam, another biology major, who never expected he'd be my co-author for many books. I taught general science for a year, while he finished his degree, and then it was my turn to stay home. That's when I wrote my first story.

We were counting pennies just to pay the rent, and I had found a children's magazine that paid $25 for a short story. How hard could it be to write a short story? I wouldn't even have to leave the house. I put our first son down for a nap and typed "The Adventures of Sammy Snake." Unknowingly, I was following the rule of "write what you know."

> How hard could it be to write a short story? I wouldn't even have to leave the house.

My story came back quickly with a curt rejection slip. I was too embarrassed to tell anyone, but the idea of writing had taken root. I signed up for a writing class in the adult education program at the local high school, and began to learn the craft of writing.

Life became more hectic because we had three more sons. I didn't have much spare time, but I did sell a few funny verses to magazines, and I won contests that required a paragraph about a specific subject. For a while, it was enough to feed my itch to write. Then one summer, while keeping an eye on four little boys, I wrote chapter one of a children's book, about two kids who volunteered in a zoo reptile house, in my stiff new black-and-white marbled notebook.

I knew nothing about publishers, but I went to the library, found a list, and mailed my manuscript to the first one. The editor liked it! But there was a hitch: Apparently it would have a wider readership with one boy and one girl character. Would I rewrite it? Of course I would! It never occurred to me that anyone would ask for a complete revision without fully intending to buy the manuscript, but I learned that lesson the hard way. A book is not sold until you've signed a contract. In the end, *Whistle For Danger* was published by Rand McNally when Peggy was two years old.

When our oldest son was approaching college age, I got a job at the Buffalo Museum of Science, in charge of school tours and Saturday classes. I had always wished that kids could see the best parts of the museum, where curators worked in the labs among stored collections of insects, study skins, and artifacts. So I decided to give kids second best—a book called *Behind These Doors: Science Museum Makers*.

One year the museum offered a "back to nature" class for adults. My co-workers and I made soap, cooked weeds, and learned to use natural dyes. When someone asked if we'd show her how to make cornhusk dolls, we thought, "How hard can that be?" We couldn't find any books to show us how, but we found a woman who was an expert.

When a craft book publisher's catalog came across my desk, I noticed that they didn't have a book on cornhusk dolls. I wrote to the editor and enclosed a sample of my writing, and a few days later he called. "I have a manuscript here," he said, "but it's not very well written. Could you complete a manuscript in a month?" I took a deep breath and said yes. With my friend and co-worker, Patricia Phibbs, we stalked the cornfields, gathered husks, soaked them, and created dozens of dolls to photograph for the book. We made the deadline!

A few years later, a teacher in an all-girls school asked me to speak to her class about women scientists. There were many to choose from, but I narrowed it down to those who worked with or studied animals. After all that research, I wrote *Wild Animals, Gentle Women*. I wrote only eight books before my sixtieth birthday. Since then, I've written three dozen more.

Nature or Nurture? Peggy's Beginning

I witnessed the birth of all but the first of my mother's books. I was gestating at the time *Whistle For Danger* was written. And like most kids, I became so familiar with my mother's career that it was no big deal when a new book came out. That was just Mom's job.

You can make an argument either way as to whether becoming a writer is due to nature or nurture. I think it's a little of both. It's in my genes, obviously, but I also grew up exposed to the smell of Wite-Out and the click clack of my mother's typewriter keys.

In many ways I grew up in my mother's books. When she wrote *Behind These Doors: Science Museum Makers*, she revealed a place that I considered my own personal secret. When she worked on Saturdays, I tagged along. After hours, I had the place to myself. I tiptoed through the Hall of Dinosaurs and paused, breathless, to listen for the faintest creak of bones coming alive. I wandered up to the third floor to watch the taxidermist skin a deer, its tawny hide peeled back to reveal pearly muscle and graying ligaments that surrounded the lifeless eye. I walked a fox on a leash, and I gritted my teeth when a two-toed sloth clung to my arm. I picked tiny milkweed pods for her "Eat the Weeds" class, and I made endless assortments of cornhusk dolls.

The museum was a special place for us because we both had wanted to be explorers. And in a sense we are. As writers we drag the hide of an obscure fact out of the jungle of information to show the world its existence. Our discoveries do not reside in dimly lit halls of science, but fill the pages of books where future explorers can discover them, too.

> The museum was a special place for us because we both had wanted to be explorers. And in a sense we are.

As a kid I always wrote. But my first published piece was a 200-word essay for a contest in *Glamour* magazine. Seeing my name in print, I was hooked. I thought, "This is easy." But publishing a second time was more difficult. So I put those efforts aside and worked on my master's degree in anthropology. While typing the first draft of my thesis, I went into labor with my daughter. One look at my tiny Kate and I knew I wanted to be a stay-at-home mom. Playing in the sandbox, eating PB&J, and making up nonsense songs became my favorite occupations. But when a chance to write a book came along, I leapt at it.

Mom was writing a book about avalanches for a series on natural disasters. The author of the volcano book dropped the project, leaving the editor in the lurch. Did my mother know another writer who could finish the job? Yes. Without much previous experience or clips to show, I was sent a contract for my first book. A miracle.

Although they deny it, I can only imagine that the editor and my mother made a deal that if I messed up, my mother would make it right. I'm happy to say she didn't have to. I learned the book business the hard way—on the fly. But I learned how to write the best way possible, as an apprentice, one-on-one with a professional writer at my side. My mother read the first draft, making polite but strongly recommended suggestions to keep my writing active and strong. Since then, I have published more than a dozen books, but I still feel as if I'm learning something new about writing, about the business, and about myself every day. With the publication of this book, I'm proud to have you learn as I have—with my mother's voice in your ear.

Chapter 1

Defining the Nonfiction Species

Nonfiction Markets

A Body of Knowledge

The Nonfiction Writer

Industry Awards

"Nonfiction writing is a state of mind, a way of life . . . a key that can open many doors, an introduction to fascinating people, a guide to wonderful adventures . . . a way to reach out to readers and to the world."
—John M. Wilson, author of *The Complete Guide to Magazine Article Writing*

I was talking to a third-grade class about one of my books when I realized why I love to write nonfiction. The book we were discussing was about animal intelligence, and I had been telling the story of meeting chimpanzees who had learned to count and use a computer. "And Kermit, one of the oldest chimps," I said, "is learning fractions!"

A ripple of giggles went around the room. One skeptical boy muttered, "Is that really true?"

When I assured him that I had met Kermit, and watched this big chimpanzee follow instructions to choose one half and then one fourth of an apple, the boy said, "Oh wow!"

It is that "oh wow" factor that gives me a thrill when I learn something I didn't know before, or find a fact that hasn't been written about in a children's book. Truth and reality are the heart and soul of nonfiction. A nonfiction writer may not always find something new, but the challenge can be finding a new way of explaining or showing an aspect of history, art, music, nature, science, or biography.

Underwear and Hot Water Tanks

Fiction is fun because anything can happen. Authors of fiction build a world. They create the place, the people, the conversation, and all the action. But nonfiction authors have to stick to reality. Our goal is to show a real world, with real people and events that sometimes seem too amazing to be real, like chimpanzees doing fractions or a man mailing himself to freedom.

> Truth and reality are the heart and soul of nonfiction.

Nonfiction may sound like a nonentity, but it is quite the opposite. It is every true story, from the life of a single atom to the construction of a pyramid or the making of a movie. It is our past and our present; every person who ever lived, every plant and animal, every game played, every bridge built, and every inventive thought. Nonfiction authors will never run out of true stories to tell.

Still, some readers tend to put nonfiction books in the category of underwear and hot water tanks—things you buy only when you need them. Many nonfiction writers don't even like the word *nonfiction* because of this negative connotation. John McPhee, a prolific nonfiction author of dozens of fascinating books for adults, calls it "literature of fact," and Newbery winner Russell Freedman has referred to himself as a factual author.

Actually, nonfiction is a special craft. Jean Fritz, who is famous for her wonderful children's biographies, believes that the art of nonfiction is using facts to make up a form. It is not a matter of coaxing up a story, she says, but of perceiving the story line that's already there.

In *Worlds of Childhood: The Art and Craft of Writing for Children*, William Zinsser compiled the speeches of six prize-winning authors of both fiction and nonfiction children's books. In the introduction he wrote, "If writers of children's books had to take an oath it might begin, 'First tell the truth'. . . . Children are tougher than adults think they are, and considerably wiser. They know when they are being lied to, condescended to, equivocated with; they know a fudged fact when they see one."

McPhee would add to that: "Whatever you are writing, your motive is always to tell a good story while you're sitting around the cave in front of the fire, before going out to club another mastodon." And nowhere is storytelling more important than in children's books.

Because Peggy and I were both science majors we came to think of nonfiction writing as a body of knowledge, and we have attempted to carefully dissect it into its working parts. Nonfiction is a simple beast, really. In its most basic form it consists of a skeleton of accurate information, the flesh and blood of story, the heart of the writer, and the muscle of marketing. Subspecies have been identified—biography, how-to, and science—but their survival and success depends on these basics.

> In this fast-paced world, a fact has a half-life of only eight years.

At a library conference in Newark, New York, information technologist Stephen Abrams surprised us when he announced that, in this fast-paced world, a fact has a half-life of only eight years. So it is critical to build your framework or skeleton of facts with the most up-to-date information you can find. The more solid your framework the more validity you and your nonfiction have.

Many of us have suffered through classes that used dull, colorless textbooks that squeezed out much of the human experience from history, scientific discovery, or technological innovations. The drippings from this thorough laundering are the flesh and blood of story—the struggle, courage, and heartache. It is the nonfiction writer's job to tell this story, to put flesh back on the bone. And thumping away in the center of the nonfiction creation is the writer's heart, the passion for her subject. Her choice of words and tone of presentation reveal the writer's concern and point of view.

The nonfiction beast would never see the light of day if not for the muscle of marketing. It takes effort to find the right home, the right publisher, for nonfiction. However, the population of children's nonfiction is huge. It is the most sought-after form of reading. If a fifth grader needs to write a report about Brazil, she grabs a nonfiction book. If a boy has a passion for dinosaurs he zeroes in on the 500s section of the nonfiction shelves in the children's library. When teens need a current event to share in class, they download an article from *Time* or the *New York Times* online. Need to repair your bike? Read a service manual. Have a health concern? Read a medical journal. Making cookies? Pull out your cookbook. For each niche in nonfiction there is a need for strong writers who are passionate about their topic, whether it is kites, kayaks, kickboxing, or curing cancer.

Creative Nonfiction

When the term "creative nonfiction" crept into the national vocabulary it caused grimaces from many writers who felt they had been creatively writing nonfiction for decades. The criticism was that "creative" suggested fiction or made up "facts." But writer and Editor Lee Gutkind, who first used the term in the 1970s, said that creative nonfiction is an umbrella term for nonfiction that "employs techniques like scene, dialogue, description, while allowing personal point of view and voice (reflection) rather than maintaining the sham of objectivity." Using this definition, Truman Capote was writing creative nonfiction when he wrote *In Cold Blood* in 1965. "What I am trying to achieve," said Capote, "is a voice while sitting by a fireplace telling you a story on a winter's evening."

When the *Los Angeles Times* Festival of Books brought together a group of nonfiction writers to discuss this new category, they generally agreed that "creative" was not the exact word they would use for the craft, but explained it as the "story" behind the facts. It is a narrative that reveals the facts of an event, such as a person's life or accomplishments, a discovery, a natural disaster, or perhaps an animal's life. The writer is the narrator.

While Gutkind might prefer the author to be vividly present in first-person narration, the panelists felt that even if a text isn't written in first person, the author is always present. One of the panelists said it is like seeing the world, not as a tourist, but focused through the lens of a camera. Orville Schell, author of *Virtual Tibet*, summed it up this way: "The writers who do creative nonfiction well know how to sit and look and describe, paint the scene." They show the place, the people, the setting in that moment, versus reporting news after the fact.

Another mistake is thinking that creative nonfiction is a genre. Instead it should be thought of as a technique. Peggy and I feel that creative nonfiction is just good nonfiction and what all nonfiction writers should strive for. Whenever possible, utilize dialogue, description, setting, and characters to inform, explain, and tell a true story. Your presence will be apparent in the text through your choice of words, your cadence, and your voice.

Claudette Colvin: Twice Toward Justice by Phillip Hoose is a prime example of creative nonfiction. Hoose captures scenes, uses dozens of quotes as dialogue, and even lets the reader hear the sound of the jail cell door clang shut. Deborah Heiligman achieves the same intimacy in *Charles and Emma: The Darwins' Leap of Faith*. Creative nonfiction is not only for biography. Read one or more science books by Sy Montgomery. She uses the same tools. "Sam Marshall is lying on his belly in the rainforest, his freckled face just inches from a fist-sized hole in the dirt. He turns on his headlamp. He gently pokes a twig into the tunnel and wiggles it. 'Come out!' he says into the hole. 'I want to meet you!'" And so begins Montgomery's *The Tarantula Scientist*.

The Nonfiction Writer

Nonfiction writers come from all walks of life. Hope Marston was an elementary school librarian before she turned to writing. The idea for her first book, *Big Rigs*, came to her because the boys at her school were always looking for easy-to-read books about big trucks. Timothy Burke was a tugboat captain operating in Lake Erie's Buffalo Harbor. After hundreds of students visited the tug, he wrote *Tugboats in Action*. Carol Johmann was a research biologist before she wrote her first how-to science book for children; Steve Swinburne was a professional photographer; and Russell Freedman was a journalist.

No matter what our backgrounds, nonfiction writers have one characteristic in common: We love to learn. In her book, *Pilgrim at Tinker Creek*, author Annie Dillard wrote, "I am no scientist, but a poet and a walker . . . with a penchant for quirky facts." That pretty much sums up most nonfiction writers too. We are perpetual students of the world soaking up the odd, unusual, bizarre, and fascinating fact. We relish hearing about heroic deeds of the past or the recent discovery of a new drug from the Amazon. But we also love to shine a light on the ordinary things of life so that they gleam in a way no one noticed before. James Cross Giblin, author and children's book editor, wrote a fascinating book on the history of silverware. Common as this subject may seem, it would be hard to resist reading his book, *Hand to Mouth: Or, How We Invented Knives, Forks, Spoons, and Chopsticks, & the Table Manners to Go With Them*.

As nonfiction writers, we do all the things that everyone else does: We walk the dog, cook breakfast, and go on vacation, but we do these things with a built-in sense of wonder. Between the dog's piddle stops, we might contemplate the bricks, cobblestones, or logs that lie under the

> No matter what our backgrounds, nonfiction writers have one characteristic in common: We love to learn.

asphalt. While cracking an egg, we might ponder the daily routine on an egg farm or how the gelatinous goo morphs into a chicken. We tend to plan our family vacations around research and interview trips.

While nonfiction writers are perpetual students, we are also eager teachers. It is no surprise that many nonfiction writers once taught or still teach in a classroom, including Susan Campbell Bartoletti, Seymour Simon, James Deem, and Jean Fritz, to name a few.

Many people have the perception that children's nonfiction is unbiased or neutral, but it is not. Good nonfiction doesn't just list cold facts, like a bedraggled witness interrogated by *Dragnet*'s Joe Friday, the straight-laced detective who was famous for the line, "Just the facts, ma'am." What that witness said was filtered through *her* eyes, *her* past experiences, and *her* personal beliefs. So, too, is everything a nonfiction writer collects, reads, and writes. Nonfiction writers are biased. We can't help it any more than anyone else can.

> Our bias is to present the facts through a hopeful lens. We portray a world where everything may not be perfect, but with hope that someday it will be better.

Our bias is to present the facts through a hopeful lens. We portray a world where everything may not be perfect, but with hope that someday it will be better. As naturalists, we could not write about the deforestation of the rainforest without talking about the efforts of coffee companies attempting to grow coffee beans in an environmentally sound manner. We need to give hope to the next generation, and perhaps inspire them into action.

Milton Meltzer, author of more than 80 biographies and histories, claimed that, "Almost everything I write has to do with social change—how it comes about, the forces that advance it and the forces that resist it, the moral issues that beset men and women seeking to realize their humanity . . . I have not been neutral; I see nothing wrong in the historian who feels a commitment to humane concerns—to the ending of war, of poverty, of racism."

Through our writing we show that there are difficulties to overcome, whether that means learning how to be a better baseball player or saving wild manatees. We provide hope and motivation by telling true stories of others who have struggled. In that respect nonfiction writers are like classroom teachers, librarians, and parents. We are committed to shaping a better world for children.

Does this description of a constant learner and hopeful teacher sound familiar? Then you may be just right for this fascinating profession of nonfiction writing.

Today's Nonfiction

Nonfiction comes in all shapes and sizes, ages and attitudes. So it is important to first understand the kinds of markets you can write for and how they differ. There are primarily four major print markets—magazines, trade books, mass-market books, and educational books—and the growing electronic market. Each has its unique benefits and all of them offer nonfiction writers plenty of opportunities to build a career.

The Magazine Market

The magazine market for or about children and young adults is made up of hundreds of magazines. This enormous market has a voracious appetite for nonfiction ideas because most magazines come out several times a year, and each issue may feature quite a few articles. This volume makes the magazine market a great place for writers to get their feet wet by crafting short, tightly focused pieces. It is also a great place to become practiced at writing about a variety of subjects. General interest magazines purchase a wide assortment of articles including biographies, craft how-to's, nature and sports; and there are specialized magazines that cater to horse fanatics, soccer players, families with twins, parents in Arizona, and nearly every other demographic you can imagine. Many magazines are also publishing online editions in addition to print, or have converted to online publication entirely.

Trade Book Market

The trade book market refers to books sold at retail in traditional bookstores, or "the trade." Trade books typically appear in hardcover with a dust jacket and, if successful, may later come out in paperback. A concentration of trade houses, such as Henry Holt, Penguin Putnam, Clarion, and Viking, are located in New York City, but today trade publishers can be found throughout the United States. Depending on the size of the company, a trade house may produce anywhere from 10 to 200 children's and young adult titles per year, half of which are nonfiction, so the competition to get on a publisher's trade list is fierce. Many houses prefer to work with authors who have agents, but it is still possible to break into this market by perfecting your craft and developing exciting ideas.

An increasing number of trade books are now being produced by book packagers. Traditional publishers are finding it more difficult to manage all aspects of their large lists in-house, so they often turn to packagers to produce books for them. These independent companies provide a variety of services: They create new book ideas; hire writers and illustrators; research photos; copyedit and proofread; do book design and page layout; and even provide printing services—essentially everything that publishers do, except for marketing, selling, and distributing the titles they produce. Because most packagers focus on producing nonfiction series titles, they offer many opportunities for freelance writers. Packagers typically look for writers with expertise in a particular subject area who can clearly demonstrate solid research and writing skills, and have the ability to meet what are often tight deadlines.

> It is still possible to break into the trade market by perfecting your craft and developing exciting ideas.

Mass Market

Mass-market books are so named because they are marketed to a large audience through chain stores, grocery stores, and airports. A typical mass-market publisher may produce more than 500 titles per year, and print many more thousands of copies of each to be sold in large volumes to their distributors. The books tend to be less expensive, paperback or jacketless hardcover, and may feature licensed characters such as SpongeBob, Mickey Mouse, or Bugs Bunny. Golden Books is a prime example of a mass-market publisher. Many large publishers have a mass-market branch. For example, Random House sells mass-market books through Ballantine. These books may also be put together by a packager and are often assigned to writers as work-for-hire projects.

The first book that Peggy and I wrote together, the *Kids' World Almanac of Amazing Facts About Numbers, Math and Money*, was produced for the mass market. It featured black and white cartoon illustrations by my son, Paul Facklam, was printed on newsprint paper, and sold in Kmart.

Educational Market

The educational market, also known as the institutional market, focuses mainly on selling curriculum-related books to schools and libraries. Educational publishers respond to the needs of teachers and librarians with titles geared to fit gaps in the market. Many nonfiction titles for the school and library market are grouped into series such as Great Americans (biographies), Cultures of the World (social studies), or Issues in Focus Today (current events). Most of the educational publishers, including Lucent Books, Facts On File, and Benchmark Books, publish only nonfiction, making this an important market for nonfiction writers. Authors who work for this market submit their resume and samples of their writing so that editors can keep them on file. New projects are usually generated in-house and given to authors on assignment.

Electronic Publishing

Electronic magazines, called e-zines, have been around for more than 15 years. Most if not all print magazines have an online counterpart that expands on or complements their print edition. Some publishers have abandoned print altogether to focus on their online presence, and many more e-zines are popping up every year. The digital world of magazines has greatly enlarged the market base for nonfiction writers, although some e-zines offer payment and some do not.

> Publishers are eager to explore the world of e-books, which is sure to expand opportunities for writers as well as readers.

The book business has been a little slower to embrace the digital world, but in 2010, Amazon announced that for the first time electronic books or e-books outsold hardcovers. Although publishers are keen to note that digital products won't replace their printed versions, they are eager to explore the world of e-books, which is sure to expand opportunities for writers as well as readers. While most book publishers got their feet wet turning tried and true titles into e-books, many are now releasing new titles in print and digital editions simultaneously. Lerner Publishing Group, for example, offers more than 1,400 nonfiction and fiction titles as e-books, including a new line called Lerner Interactive Books that allows struggling readers to adjust the reading pace and listen as the story is read. Picture books, in particular, fit perfectly in an e-book and apps format. Kids can learn about dinosaurs on Mom's cell phone while waiting for a doctor's appointment or sitting in a grocery cart. E-readers have also found a home in schools because e-textbooks are less expensive to purchase and easier to update. As the technology continues to change, the one constant will be the writers who create the content.

Although the publishing industry seems clear cut, the boundaries between these major categories have become blurred. Scholastic, for example, has a variety of imprints that produce trade books, mass-market titles, curriculum-based texts, and e-books; it also maintains a magazine for kids and classrooms. You will find many mass-market books in schools and libraries, and high-quality institutional titles in bookstores. As a nonfiction writer, it is important to know the characteristics of each market in order to be successful. You may have a wonderful idea, but is it right for a trade house or an educational publisher, or is it more appropriate as a magazine article? Do you prefer to come up with your own ideas, or would you like to get assignments? The best way to become familiar with each market is to read a variety of books and note the differences.

> A turning point for nonfiction came in 1988, when Russell Freedman won the Newbery Medal for *Lincoln: A Photobiography.*

Get to know as many children's magazines as you can. Check them out at your local library, send away for sample copies, or visit their websites. Each magazine, like each publishing house, has a unique style. Where does your writing fit best? There is always room for new writers in each type of market, and a nonfiction writer can publish in multiple markets.

From Second Class to Head of the Class

In the past, Peggy and I have gone to conferences to speak or to learn from other writers and found ourselves sitting next to fiction authors with long lines of fans waiting to have their books signed. There have been moments when we felt like the ugly stepsisters at the ball—second-class writers whose books were viewed as more function than fun.

Fortunately, the perception of nonfiction writing has changed. A turning point came in 1988, when Russell Freedman won the Newbery Medal for *Lincoln: A Photobiography*. A nonfiction title had not won the prize since 1956. Since then, several nonfiction books have garnered Caldecott and Newbery medals and honors including *So You Want to Be President?* by Judith St. George; *Claudette Colvin: Twice Toward Justice* by Phillip Hoose; *Hitler Youth: Growing Up in Hitler's Shadow* by Susan

Campbell Bartoletti; and *Moses: When Harriet Tubman Led her People to Freedom* by Carole Boston Weatherford.

Another step up the ladder of respectability occurred in 2001. The American Library Association (ALA), the organization that also awards the Newbery and Caldecott medals, inaugurated its first award solely for children's nonfiction: the Robert F. Sibert Informational Book Award. Each year it is given to the author of the most distinguished children's informational book published during the preceding year. The first honoree was Marc Aronson for his book, *Sir Walter Ralegh and the Quest for El Dorado.*

The more attention nonfiction has received, the more people have realized that it is an exciting art form that balances interesting fact with original format. These award-winning books give readers an innovative look at familiar subjects. Their authors did not regurgitate information, but processed that material through their own sensibilities and understanding to come to their own conclusions. Think of a quilt maker who follows a pattern that hundreds of other quilters have used, but works from a diverse color pallet, features an unusual background stitch, and uses textured fabric. The pattern looks familiar but it is startlingly different and stands out from the rest.

> ". . . the best writers of nonfiction put their hearts and minds into their work. Their concern is not only with what they have to say but how they say it."

The striking blend of fact and form comes when a writer invests herself in the project. Milton Meltzer believed that "the best writers of nonfiction put their hearts and minds into their work. Their concern is not only with what they have to say but how they say it." He added that if the writer cares, a feeling will emerge in the rhythm of the sentences, in the choice of details, and in the color of the language. "If the writer is indifferent, bored, stupid, or mechanical, it will show in the work. The kind of man or woman the writer is—this is what counts."

Have the writers or the writing changed that much over time, or become that much better? Probably not, but one aspect of nonfiction that has changed is the visual design. When the first DK Eyewitness books came on the market in 1988, they were a design innovation with their clean white pages, clear bright photographs, and small captions of text distributed over the page. It was one company's response to a sagging book market, and the series was successful because its new design reflected the preference of a generation raised on television and video games. Other publishers quickly borrowed from this popular look. Dorling Kindersley raised the bar for all publishers to make their nonfiction as engaging and appealing as possible. But cutting edge trends eventually become the mainstream, and publishers are constantly looking for interesting ways to design their books.

Today, the most effective designs don't follow a trend but are original and specific. They embrace the theme and subject of the text. One example is Chris Barton's book titled *The Day-Glo Brothers*, published by Charlesbridge. The illustrator, Tony Persiani, used Day-Glo colors and captured the 1950s time period in quirky retro illustrations. Another example is *The Great and Only Barnum: The Tremendous, Stupendous Life of Showman P. T. Barnum* by Candace Fleming. Barnum's flamboyance practically leaps off each page with elephant-sized fonts and circus regalia.

Nonfiction Made-to-Order

Originality in nonfiction may seem contradictory, but according to Marc Aronson, originality comes in the form of *conception*, how the author thought about the subject matter in a new way; and *organization*, how that author juxtaposed the information to be true to the subject matter and in tune with his readers. Add to that a fresh, passionate voice, insightful research strategies, and appealing design and you have nonfiction that today is the gold standard.

Too much pressure? Don't worry. Let's start at the very beginning. First you need something to write about: an idea.

Awards for Children's Writing

The Boston Globe-Horn Book Awards honors the year's best in picture books, fiction and poetry, and nonfiction.

The Caldecott Medal is presented each year by the American Library Association to the artist of the most distinguished American book for children.

CBC and NCSS Notable Social Studies Trade Books for Young People are defined as exemplary books for K-12 "that emphasize human relations, represent a diversity of groups and are sensitive to a broad range of cultural experiences."

CBC and NSTA Outstanding Science Trade Books for Students K-12 are part of a yearly round-up of books recognized for their scientific accuracy, clarity, presentation, and design. The titles are promoted in conjunction with the Children's Book Council.

The Children's Book Guild Nonfiction Award is granted to "an author or author/illustrator whose total work has contributed significantly to the quality of nonfiction for children."

Coretta Scott King Book Award, sponsored by the American Library Association, honors outstanding African American authors and illustrators whose books express and encourage the literary and artistic expression of the black experience in the U.S.

Jane Addams Children's Book Awards are given annually to books that promote the cause of peace, social justice, world community, and the equality of the sexes and all races. Categories include fiction, nonfiction, and poetry.

The Michael L. Printz Award For Excellence in Young Adult Literature honors the best books for young adults in the categories of fiction, nonfiction, poetry, and anthology. This is an annual award sponsored by the American Library Association.

(continued)

The National Book Award for Young People's Literature recognizes the best written works for children and young people each year. Sponsored by the National Book Foundation, this award is given "to writers by writers."

The Newbery Medal is awarded annually by the American Library Association to the author of the most distinguished contribution to American literature for children.

The Orbis Pictus Award for Outstanding Nonfiction for Children is sponsored by the National Council of Teachers of English. A committee selects one book as the most outstanding nonfiction work for children each year.

Parents' Choice Awards, sponsored by the Parents' Choice Foundation, are given to books that help kids grow "imaginatively, physically, morally, and socially."

The Robert F. Sibert Informational Book Award, sponsored by the American Library Association, recognizes the author and illustrator of the year's most distinguished informational book. It considers clarity and accuracy of the text and illustrative material, as well as appropriate documentation, distinctive use of language, and excellent artistic presentation in illustration.

SCBWI Golden Kite Awards annually recognize excellence in children's literature. They are given to published authors and illustrators in four categories: fiction, nonfiction, picture book text, and picture book illustration.

The SCBWI Magazine Merit Awards are presented by the Society of Children's Book Writers and Illustrators in recognition of outstanding original magazine work created by SCBWI members for young people in the areas of fiction, nonfiction, poetry, and illustration.

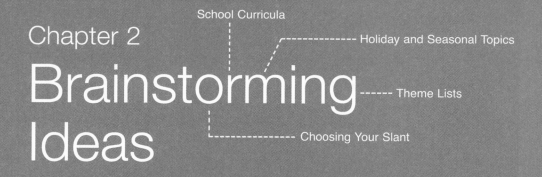

Chapter 2
Brainstorming Ideas

School Curricula

Holiday and Seasonal Topics

Theme Lists

Choosing Your Slant

"One of the things that happens when you give yourself permission to start writing is that you start thinking like a writer. You start seeing everything as material."

—Anne Lamott, author of *Bird by Bird*

There is a general rule of thumb in writing: Write what you know. But if that were the case when we began to write, we might have only written about our activities at the time—PTA and diapers—or our preparental interests—snakes and bones.

"Write what you know" seems too limiting. Lee Wyndham's book, *Writing for Children and Teenagers*, says, "Write what you know . . . Pooh! If the 'rules' of writing were hard and fast, maybe the craft would be easier to practice." She points out that Jules Verne never traveled 20,000 leagues under the sea, nor did Edgar Rice Burroughs see Africa before he wrote *Tarzan of the Apes*.

We didn't know everything about numbers, math, and money before we researched the *Kids' World Almanac of Amazing Facts about Numbers, Math, and Money*, and we can't imagine that David Macaulay knew how everything worked before he wrote his best-selling book, *The Way Things Work*. Or that Jim Giblin knew all about windows before he wrote *Let There Be Light*. We all had a spark of interest and a curiosity that would not be satisfied until we committed ourselves to the project. So our motto is this: Write what you are curious or passionate about.

Phillip Hoose, author of *The Race to Save the Lord God Bird* and winner of the 2005 Boston Globe-Horn Book Award, reminded the audience in his acceptance speech that "most good stories, fiction or nonfiction, contain the same elements: characters you care about, intriguing relationships between and among them, suspense, difficult obstacles, and a good setting. So, because I have a special love for birds, and to write about the work that I do, I set out to find a Clark Gable of a bird and a *Gone with the Wind* of a story." Writing about his passion, the elusive Ivory-billed Woodpecker, paid off. Not only did Hoose win a coveted award, but readers everywhere could share in his enthusiasm.

> Our motto is this: Write what you are curious or passionate about.

Nonfiction writing is one job that gives you permission to explore your whims and satisfy your curiosity. "What I like about nonfiction," says Jan Fields, author of dozens of magazine articles and editor of *Kid Magazine Writers* e-zine, "is the ability to use what I am interested in at that moment. When I learned about an interesting kind of butterfly, I researched it for the sake of my own curiosity but then wrote an article about it to share the cool stuff." You can do the same. What interests you?

A World of Ideas

We've already mentioned writing about your passions, and perhaps you already have. But there may be a limited market for your particular interest. How many books or articles does the world need on buttons of the

Civil War Era? Unless you don't mind being a one-book wonder, you may have to broaden your scope.

Most of the nonfiction writers we know think that getting ideas is the easiest part of their job. They have more ideas than time to write. How do ideas come so easily to them, while others flounder with writer's block?

The concept of "getting an idea" sounds as if you can go to a kiosk at the mall and purchase one, but it really is a state of awareness combined with the practice of creativity. You have to be conscious of the world around you and innovative in adapting a well-worn topic and turning it into an eye-catching story.

Story Alert

Marilyn Helmer, author of several picture books and riddle books for Kids Can Press, says, "I have trained myself to constantly be on *story alert.*" She has honed the skill of seeing the potential story in the things she does, places she goes, and events she reads about or sees on TV. Her file drawers are overflowing with articles clipped from newspapers and magazines on things she might like to write about someday.

> Your job as a nonfiction writer is to raise your antenna and tune in to the true stories that exist around you.

Ideas are everywhere. Your job as a nonfiction writer is to raise your antenna and tune in to the true stories that exist around you. One way to do this is to keep your own idea file. Like Helmer, Peggy and I have folders filled with articles clipped from newspapers and magazines. My editor, Barbara Lucas, occasionally sends me clippings from New York City with a nudging word or two in the margin: "interesting" or "something to think about." My clippings tend to be from the science section of the newspaper, but yours might be current events, places of interest, recipes, or feature articles about a local hero or villain.

Peggy's idea file consists of an odd assortment of pages including a clipping about the world's largest pumpkin, another about a rare white bear, a file card that says ARCHAEO-ASTRONOMY, directions to play an animal guessing game, notes about a place called Hawk Creek, and a short scribbled list of animals that throw up. If you visited her office, you'd see more scraps of paper taped to the walls and dozens of books flagged with post-its holding an idea in place.

Train yourself to be on "story alert" by carrying a small notebook so you can jot down an idea that comes to you when you are away from home. Or borrow Anne Lamott's file card system. In her book *Bird by Bird*, Lamott encourages writers to keep a single file card in their pocket, purse, bedside table, and glove compartment. It is also easy to jot down an idea on your cell phone using the notes function or email an idea to yourself so that when you get home you can add it to a file folder on your computer. There are also software programs like Scrivener or Character Keeper that keep ideas organized.

Whatever your system, it doesn't have to be fancy or official. Use what is at hand. Once, on a family vacation to Mount Vernon, Peggy was so struck with the idea of writing about George Washington's penchant for farming that she spent all her time scribbling notes in the margins of the brochure and map as she wandered through rows of cabbage and crookneck squash. When you start writing your ideas down you will find yourself looking at the world differently. You will begin to see everything in life as a story.

We also recommend writing ideas down not because we doubt your long-term memory capacity, but ideas, like good chicken stock, need to simmer. Nonfiction author Mel Boring used to say that ideas were gems in a treasure chest, but over the years, he admitted that his analogy changed. A treasure chest implies that ideas are polished and perfect right away. They aren't. They are raw, lacking form and structure. Boring better described the process as cultivating a garden where an idea is small and indistinguishable at first, but with mulching and tending it grows into a great book or article.

So occasionally review your stash of ideas. Are any of the thoughts you jotted down days or months ago ready to develop? The ideas that continue to nag at you are ready to be written. One year after her visit to Mount Vernon, Peggy finished an article for *Cricket* magazine on George Washington's farming prowess, and three years after that, she sold the 48-page picture book manuscript to Calkins Creek for what would become *Farmer George Plants a Nation*.

Top Five Inspiration Locations

Ideas stew in the subconscious, mingling with other thoughts as you go through the day. At the oddest moments they flash into your consciousness, breaking a bout of writer's block or solidifying a new project. We asked nonfiction writers where they get their flashes of inspiration. Five of the most common answers were:

1. In the car
2. Washing dishes
3. In church
4. Taking a walk
5. Just before sleep

Ask the Professionals

To fine-tune your story antenna, enlist the help of professionals. Ask your local children's librarian what kinds of books are lacking on the nonfiction shelves. What subjects are kids scrambling for? Your librarian will tell you there is a clear gender difference. Boys gravitate to books about dinosaurs, rockets, racing cars, and sports, while girls often choose books about pets, horses, crafts, music, and dance.

These subjects are perennial, but some related facts change every year. Do any of these books need updating? A large public library replaces titles about science, geography, technology, and social issues every five years or so. Look on the shelf and see what topics need to be written about with a fresh eye and new research.

Talk to teachers. Learn about the national curriculum standards and the specific curricula for individual states. In New York State, for example, every fourth grader learns about the Erie Canal, so targeting that age level would be a smart move if you have a passion for that particular man-made body of water. All middle-school students in North Dakota learn to compare works of art from different historical periods, so a new mid-grade book on the subject might be useful. As you look at each state's standards you will notice that most of the subjects cross state lines. Are there ample resources for each subject at the proper reading level?

School Curricula and Magazine Needs

Teachers and librarians often turn to magazines to supplement school studies or lure reluctant readers to explore age-appropriate subjects. "*Cobblestone* is often used in schools as an alternative to textbooks," says Editor Meg Chorlian, "so we take great pains to provide historically accurate articles as well as interesting ways of presenting them to our readers." Because teachers and librarians are such important consumers of magazines, editors keep their needs in mind as they plan age-appropriate themes. One way they do this is through connections with school curricula.

First grade. Social science for first graders, for example, compares aspects of life today to life long ago (classrooms, modes of transportation, etc.). First graders also learn about national holidays and how a good citizen behaves. Early Reader texts often discuss getting along with others and introduce unusual holidays. Science for first graders explores what defines life, the diversity of life, weather, and the states of matter and how they change; interesting facts about animals are popular nonfiction topics.

Third grade. Third graders look at local history and the contribution of individual heroes to America's past. They also examine Native American cultures. Articles featuring authentic Native American (or other cultural) elements are popular, as are biographies that focus on how one person can make a big difference. In science, third graders study conservation, how organisms adapt to survive, energy (especially light), and our solar system. One thing you won't see in magazines, however, is a basic primer on the solar system—magazines want to enhance and supplement, not rehash material from children's textbooks.

Fifth grade. Fifth-grade science focuses on systems and how things function: living things and their internal structure, the water cycle, atomic theory and how atoms form molecules that form elements that form organisms and other things. History for this age level is more linear: the age of exploration and colonial government. Fifth graders also spend more time looking at geography and how geography and climate affect people's lives. At this age, kids learn states and capitals. Popular articles for fifth graders often feature little-known figures in American history. Science articles look at how things work and how individuals fit into functioning relationships.

Eighth grade. Eighth-grade students study how government works and times when it has failed to work. They examine the development of democracy through primary documents such as the Magna Carta, the English Bill of Rights, and the Mayflower Compact. They also learn about economies and how they differed historically in various regions. Articles for this age often include a strong regional element. In science, eighth graders are introduced to physics (velocity), chemistry (the elements), the universe, and how chemistry is a component of biology. Science articles for this age explore these theories and include fairly complex chemistry experiments and activities.

Many public libraries carry school curricula information in their reference departments, and an Internet search on "school curriculum" will bring up grade-related guidelines from different schools. Reading through school curricula will help you better connect your ideas with the right reader age and generate article ideas that have special appeal to editors.

Look at book publishers' catalogs to see what they *haven't* published yet. Search for gaps. For example, if a publisher's series of multicultural craft books is missing one about your native land, perhaps that's a potential query.

The same goes for magazines. Scan through the issues of the last three years of a magazine and list the subjects covered. What subjects are missing? What topics might be expanded, and which are worth doing again? Each year magazines address recurring themes such as seasons and holidays. Everyone writes about Christmas and Halloween, but there are dozens of lesser-known holidays that you could write about, such as Chinese New Year, Ramadan, or Arbor Day. These topics are especially attractive to editors if they have a curriculum connection.

Submitting Holiday and Seasonal Material

Magazine editors occupy a different time continuum from the rest of us. While we're looking for the first signs of spring on chilly March mornings, the editors at *Girls' Life* are thinking about fun in the summer sun, editors at *Humpty Dumpty* are choosing the best Thanksgiving craft, and editors at *Fun for Kidz* are exploring back-to-school topics. If you send your great spring story to any of these editors, you'll catch them out of sync with their magazine's editorial schedule. So how do you time your seasonal and holiday material to meet editors' needs?

With some magazines, it's fairly easy. *Highlights*, *Pockets*, and *Boys' Quest*, for example, stockpile articles for months (or years) into the future, so they're less influenced by the timing of an article's arrival. Still, the most common rule for seasonal material is to send it six to eight months before

--the targeted time of year. This catches magazine editors at their most receptive moments.

You will also get a better response if you avoid a clichéd approach to seasonal topics. Most magazines, for instance, have an over-abundance of snow articles. Writers love writing about snow, but many editors specifically ask for material that shows the non-snowy side of winter. Make an editor smile by brainstorming new ways to greet each season.

Before submitting holiday articles, carefully examine your target market, especially when writing about religious holidays. Magazines have definite policies about how to handle such holidays, and some prefer not to mention them at all. Often these preferences are not explained in writers' guidelines. You can only learn about them by examining specific issues and seeing how the magazine has handled holidays in the past. For example, *Our Little Friend* does not use stories about Santa Claus, Halloween, or the Easter Bunny. *Jack and Jill* will accept puzzles and activities that mention Santa, and prefers holiday stories that are more historical, cultural, or social rather than religious.

When considering a holiday or seasonal piece, choose elements that are unusual or unexpected. Material that is fresh and surprising is sure to make any editor celebrate.

Take advantage of inside information. Each month, valuable resources like *Children's Writer* newsletter (www.childrenswriter.com); the Society of Children's Book Writers and Illustrators newsletter (www.scbwi.org); the *Bulletin of the Center for Children's Books* (http://bccb.lis.Illinois.edu); *Kid Magazine Writers* (www.kidmagwriters.com); and dozens of literary blogs and websites supply submission guidelines and information about what editors are looking for.

Magazine Theme Lists

Many magazines focus each issue around a theme and post the upcoming themes on their websites. What a gift. Magazine editors have saved you from that dreaded question, "What should I write about?"—at least for a moment or two. Writer Marilyn Freeman considers a theme list to be "the next best thing to having your mom in the publishing business." With a list in hand, you know what editors are looking for—now you just have to write it.

Check the theme lists frequently, many of which can be found online, for updates or additions. Timing is everything. Your manuscript submission or query must be on the editor's desk at least eight months prior to the targeted issue. However, the social studies magazine *Appleseeds* requests that queries be dated ten to eleven months in advance. So if hats are the theme for a February issue, you should have your query letter written and submitted by the previous March. If you uncover startling new information about fedoras a month later, it is too late for that particular issue. Don't beat yourself up if you miss a theme for which you had the perfect article or idea. Magazines often reprise a theme within two or three years.

> Timing is everything. Your submission must be on the editor's desk at least eight months prior to the targeted issue.

When looking at a theme list, don't forget to also look at past issues to gauge style and content. Don't overlook the ordinary. At *Know* magazine, Editor Adrienne Mason gives writers free rein on how they approach a topic, but she says, "In the end, I want clear writing that is factually correct with a light, fun touch as well."

Not inspired by theme lists? Follow author Peggy King Anderson's advice. In an online article on her website, www.peggyking.com, "Writing To Theme," Anderson suggests jump-starting your inspiration with idea lists. She recommends posting the theme in four places such as the refrigerator, the bathroom mirror, the bedside table, and your favorite chair. Each time you pass by jot down what comes to mind. At the end of two or three days, gather your lists and brainstorm on the computer. Anderson has found that this method allows her to incubate the theme subconsciously, creating spontaneous inspiration in the same way that a seeded oyster develops a lustrous cultured pearl.

An Editor's Idea

A growing number of publishing companies market to schools and libraries, advertising books for every possible course. These curriculum-driven publishers have a list of topics they need people to cover. "Our marketing and research departments monitor curriculum changes," says Chandra Howard, senior acquisitions editor for four Gale imprints, including Lucent Books. "We also use librarian focus groups to provide feedback on specific title needs." Any new titles that Lucent produces are chosen based on the titles that are already selling well, and on changes in curriculum. "If there are subject gaps in the market," Howard says, "we try to fill them."

Like a magazine theme list, the advantage of getting an assignment from an editor is that it eliminates the guesswork of what editors want. The writer makes the connection with the editor first so there is no work up front, no researching your topic to find just the right focus. It also eliminates the long process of sending out query letters and proposals to prospective editors and waiting for replies.

But assignment writing may diminish some of the excitement that comes with an author-driven title. The writer might not be passionate about the project. When Peggy took on the assignment of writing about artificial intelligence, for example, it was difficult for her to sustain the curiosity for things mechanical. Her heart wasn't in it, and that made it more difficult to write an engaging manuscript. To keep her enthusiasm up, she worked overtime looking for stories that excited her, so she could make the subject more interesting for the reader, too.

On the other hand, you might fall in love with a topic you weren't familiar with. Peggy had never heard of Grace Hopper until she was assigned to write her biography. Hopper turned out to be a fascinating and feisty woman, and a pioneering mathematician who wrote some of the first computer programs in a male-dominated field. Her innovative approach to problem-solving led her to work at the Pentagon, eventually becoming the first female rear admiral of the U.S. Navy.

In order to break into writing series books for the educational market, it's a good idea to keep clippings of your published work and develop a track record for writing in a specific field. When Howard receives writers' resumes she looks at their educational background and their list of publications. She prefers to work with writers who have written for a series before, but she admits to hiring a handful of writers who had not yet been published.

A subject may have been written about, but not by *you*—not with your ideas, and not from your perspective.

Once you get that assignment or develop an original idea, it is up to you to decide how to approach the material. That is where creativity comes in. You'll need to find a fresh way to present the information, or, in writer's terms, give it a new slant.

What's Your Slant?

The curse of nonfiction writers is that little voice that says, "Oh, that's already been done." If that were the case, then most nonfiction writers would be out of a job, and the ones left would report only on new discoveries. A subject may have been written about, but not by *you*—not with your ideas, and not from your perspective.

Among the hundreds of books written about caterpillars and butterflies for elementary school children, the author list includes veteran writers like myself, as well as Laurence Pringle and Jim Arnosky. But each of us took a different approach. I wrote about the larval stage in *Creepy Crawly*

Caterpillars; Pringle focused on just one butterfly in *Monarch*; and Arnosky wrote a field guide in *Crinkleroot's Guide to Knowing Butterflies & Moths*.

The key to having a "good idea" is how you approach your subject. You may take a broad overview or focus on something narrower. For example, Peggy's *Talking Bones* paints an extensive picture of all that forensic anthropologists do, how the science got started, and what it entails. Her biographical article on George Washington, on the other hand, focuses narrowly on one aspect of his life as a farmer.

One way to define your focus more specifically is to talk it out. What is your story about? Nonfiction author Po Bronson says that he calls up his assistant and tries to explain what he is writing about in five or ten minutes. He relies on the fact that he will naturally shape the story into its basic components as he relates it out loud.

I try to write the copy for the book jacket, or a sentence or two about the article. If I can't describe the idea concisely, I haven't found my focus yet. Barbara Lucas, who was a wonderful editor for many years, likens it to winding one strand of pasta on your fork from a plateful of spaghetti. That one strand is the focus.

On a school visit to Brumsted Elementary in Holland, New York, Peggy led students through a brainstorming session to demonstrate one method of narrowing your focus. The task was to come up with as many ways as possible to write about sneakers. One class came up with 23 ideas. They used the journalist's basic tools of who, what, where, when, why, and how. Who invented sneakers? Why? Who designs sneakers? What are sneakers made of? How many rubber trees does it take to make the soles on one pair of sneakers, or how many pairs of sneakers can you get out of one tree? Where are the majority of sneakers made? How long does it take to make a pair? When did sneakers become fashionable? Who collects sneakers and how many pairs do they have? How many kinds of sneakers are there? Just about any subject can be approached through an historic perspective, a geographical standpoint, a technological angle, or a biographical focus.

The Frankenstein Factor

The beauty of nonfiction is that you can recycle your research by using what we like to call the Frankenstein Factor. Take portions of your research and give them new life. Look at what you have written about before and see if you can find new ways to present the information.

The famous old Galapagos tortoise, Lonesome George, was the subject of a chapter in my book called *And Then There Was One*, about animals in danger of becoming extinct. Later, he was the subject of an article in *Ranger Rick*, in which I focused on how the tortoises' eggs are put in an incubator, and when they hatch, the baby tortoises are returned to their native island. Peggy has also taken advantage of the Frankenstein Factor. A portion of her book, *Bird Alert*, was excised away and crafted into a newspaper article featuring the eagle-cams and naturalists at Iroquois National Wildlife Refuge.

The key to writing more than one manuscript about the same subject is change. Change your lead, change your target audience, change your slant, narrow your focus or broaden it. Each publication has a different style, and by altering your lead, you can make your story more appealing to individual editors. In her article, "Recycle Research to Rethink & Resell Ideas," Lizann Flatt uses two examples from Fiona Bayrock's writing that illustrate the importance of using a new lead that fits a magazine's style. Bayrock matched the fun style of *Yes Magazine* by starting her article on spiny lobsters with "What do spiny lobsters play—violin or guitar?" She then pitched a similar article to *Highlights* magazine, called "How Lobsters Make Music," with a different lead: "Dr. Sheila Patek is a scientist who studies how animals talk to each other. She is curious about spiny lobsters." Each article goes on to offer the same basic information, but in two distinct styles.

> Change your lead, change your target audience, change your slant, narrow your focus or broaden it.

Although many book contracts contain a clause that prevents you from writing another book that will compete with the original one, it is fine to simplify your text and write for a much younger audience, or expand on your subject and write for a much older reader. The difference will again involve altering your writing style. An older child appreciates and understands complex sentence structures, technical or specialized jargon, and sophisticated metaphors and analogies, while a younger reader needs clear and precise language, and simpler vocabulary and sentences.

Changing your slant is another option. If you wrote about a boy who was trapped by an avalanche then rescued by a dog, perhaps in another article you can feature the dog and its handler and how rescue dogs are trained. Author Mary Meinking recycled research she did on George Washington's athletic ability. "My first article was about GW as a boy athlete, used in *Appleseeds*. Then I focused on Washington's horseback-riding ability . . . selling it to *Wee Ones*." Another time she recycled research that was used for an article about slave labor on cocoa plantations: while one article had a child labor theme, the other focused on chocolate. All it took was a little reconfiguration.

> An older child appreciates and understands complex sentence structures, technical or specialized jargon, and sophisticated metaphors and analogies.

If you have written a book, how could it be divided up into several articles? A broad topic such as the history of computers could be segmented into the first chess-playing computers, early robots, and high-tech gadgets of today. Conversely, have you written several articles with a unifying theme? Perhaps they could be joined together to form the backbone of a book.

Nonfiction for Every Age Level

When you are developing your idea, it is helpful to know how publishers categorize their products for different readers, and what the requirements for each category are. The age of the child dictates the tone and length of the text. The best way to get a feel for where your writing fits in is to read a variety of books and magazines from each basic category. In the following chart, we have used some of our own book titles as examples.

Age of Reader	Books	Magazines
Preschool (0-5)	**Board books:** 8-12 pages. Introduce simple concepts like colors, shapes, and animals. **Example:** *I Eat Dinner*— Using only 76 words, it introduces how different animals eat. **Picture books:** Less than 1,000 words. Explore a child's world. **Example:** Rookie Toddler books	Nonfiction articles are limited to concepts encountered in a child's life. 500 words or less, written in a casual tone. **Examples:** *Babybug*, *Turtle*, *High Five*
Elementary (5-8)	**32-page Picture books:** 1,500 words or less. Text and illustrations share equally in telling the story. Wide range of subject matter. **Example:** *The Big Bug Book* **48-page Picture books:** May contain up to 3,000 words, intended for older readers. **Example:** *Farmer George Plants a Nation*	Articles tend to be general interest in subjects such as crafts, nature, science, history, and sports. The tone of the writing is casual and fun. Word count is typically between 500 and 800 words. **Examples:** *Time for Kids*, *Highlights for Children*, *Spider*

Age of Reader	Books	Magazines
Elementary (5-8) ----	**Easy readers:** Transitional books for children who are reading but are not ready for chapter books. Limited vocabulary and simple sentence structure. 48-64 pages, up to 1,500 words. **Examples:** Book lines such as Rookie Readers, Step Into Reading, I Can Read!	
Middle-grade (8-12) -------	**Chapter books:** 48-64 pages. Text predominates, but photos or illustrations help readers understand concepts. The text, 4,000-12,000 words, is divided into short chapters that address certain aspects of the subject, and includes a glossary, index, and other back matter. **Example:** *Reptile Rescue*	Each magazine at this age level has a specific mission and content serving a particular audience. Articles of up to 1,000 words delve deeper into subjects with a light and conversational tone. **Examples:** *American Girl, Calliope, Cobblestone, Faces, Dig, Sports Illustrated Kids*
Young adult (12-18) -------	**Chapter books:** 128 pages or more with more than 12,000 words. These titles are often written by authors with an interest or educational background in the subject matter, although it is not required. **Example:** *Forensic Anthropology: The Science of Talking Bones*	Magazines especially for this age group contain articles up to 2,000 words. High on teen appeal, articles are written in an authoritative yet never condescending tone. **Examples:** *College Outlook, Devozine, Key Club, Seventeen, Teen Times*

(continued)

Nonfiction for Every Age Level (cont.)

These categories are not hard and fast. Keep in mind that you can write a book or article about almost any subject for any age group. Take books about weather. The simple text in the 32-page picture book, *The Best Book of Weather* by Simon Adams, introduces different kinds of weather to children ages 4-7. *Wild Science Projects About Earth's Weather*, by Robert Gardner, is a 48-page book filled with simple science experiments for grades 3-4. Kathleen Simpson focuses on Earth's weather future in her 64-page middle-grade title *Extreme Weather: Science Tackles Global Warming and Climate Change*. And the expanded edition of *A Chronology of Weather*, by Michael Allaby, written for the young adult reader, recounts past weather disasters and storm tracking technology.

A Book or Article?

Part of coming up with the right idea is presenting it in the right format. Is your idea appropriate for a book or would it be a better magazine article? It could be both. In the history section of any library you will find books that cover the entire scope of the Civil War, but in a magazine there may be a single article that focuses on one general who fought for the Confederacy, or about the medical procedures of Union doctors.

The differences between a nonfiction book and a magazine article are length of text and scope of content. Mason at *Know* magazine says, "I guess fewer words would be too obvious, but that's really the issue here. You have to get right at the meat of the story and there is no room for words that don't do a job for the article."

Magazine articles have a tighter focus than books. Articles allow a writer to discuss subjects that might not have the longevity to sustain a book—a profile of a not-so-well-known actor, a regional issue, or a current event, for instance. Articles can be trendy and have popular appeal. They satisfy the reader's curiosity quickly.

To answer the book or magazine question, ask yourself how long you want to spend on the project. A book typically takes a year or more to research and write, while an article can take a considerably shorter amount of time. The publishing schedule for a magazine is speedier too. Magazines offer many more opportunities for a writer, especially a novice, to get published. Magazine editors need dozens of new articles every month whereas a book publisher may print fewer than 15 to 20 nonfiction titles a year.

The magazine market is a vast and fertile field of opportunities that sustains many nonfiction writers full time. And, if you want to make that sideways move to the book market, writing for magazines is a good way to hone your nonfiction craft. Your magazine articles will become the "clips" that you send to a book publisher as examples of your writing skills and voice.

> Magazines offer many more opportunities for a writer, especially a novice, to get published.

So, did you figure out if your idea is right for a book or article? Would you rather get a book assignment or write for a theme list? While you read this chapter, did you jot down an idea or two or twelve? Is there an old article lurking in your drawer that deserves a fresh slant to bring it back to life? Now that you know what you want to write about, you are ready to dig into the research.

What Kind of Article Are You Writing?

There are several types of nonfiction articles. Each category has a different intent or focus. So ask yourself, "What do I want my readers to experience?" Do you want them to learn something new, to participate or create, to be inspired, empathize, or moved into action? Understanding the different categories will help you choose the best presentation for your idea.

Biography: The story of a famous person, either living or dead. A biography can cover a person's entire life or focus on one incident.

Factual/informational: The purpose is to inform. Popular informational articles include those tied to school curricula and trivia pieces that reveal surprising facts in history, science, nature, health, etc.

Games/puzzles/activities: Common short fillers for many magazines. Word games and puzzles often relate to magazine content, theme, or school curricula. Science-related activities are particularly desirable.

How-to: Instructs the reader in hands-on application. How-to articles can give general steps toward lifestyle changes or detailed directions for recipes or crafts.

Interview/profile: Focuses on the experiences and ideas of a specific person or group of people. Profiles can be informative, persuasive, or inspirational.

Personal experience: Use experiences from your life to instruct, inform, persuade, or inspire.

Persuasive: Inspire action. Articles on health and social issues are often persuasive.

Photo-essays: Photos form the core; text is usually limited to long captions. Photo-essays are informational and often target younger readers.

Reviews: Another filler; less popular than the more interactive activity or puzzle. Reviews offer information and opinions on books, movies, or other media.

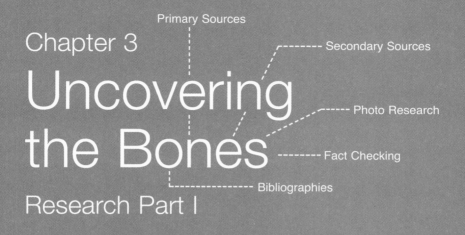

Chapter 3
Uncovering
the Bones

Primary Sources

Secondary Sources

Photo Research

Fact Checking

Bibliographies

Research Part I

"If your mother says she loves you, get a second source."

—Reporters' axiom

$\mathbf{A}$n archaeologist digs through tons of soil, sifting out tiny bone fragments that will tell the story of a past life. Like an archaeologist, a
nonfiction writer must sift through thousands of bits of information for
just the right facts that will tell the story of an entire civilization, a famous
sports figure, an animal's life cycle, or how chewing gum is made. The
facts that you uncover become the bones for your body of text, the skeleton that will hold it together.

Ancient human remains are not found just anywhere. Scientists have
to know where to search for tombs in the vast Egyptian desert. And you
must know where to look to find the facts you need. You may not even

have to leave your desk. A first-person opinion piece, for example, on how you survived an alligator attack will be filled with your own recollections of the experience. You become your own expert. You remember what the weather was like, how your heart raced as the alligator approached, and how many times you hit the gator with your paddle. But to bolster the article you may want to quote the gamekeeper who rescued you from the jaws of the giant reptile, or include a statistic about the frequency of alligator attacks. This is where research comes into play. Research can be done in any number of ways, but traditionally begins with a thorough review of print material and online sources.

Starting from Scratch

Research is much easier when you know what you are looking for and know the subject matter very well. But many nonfiction writers take on writing projects where they are learning about the topic for the first time. Peggy (who admits to being not only computer challenged but also math phobic) once took on an assignment to write about artificial intelligence. Her only experience with this subject was watching battling robots on cable TV. She had to start from scratch, asking basic questions: What is artificial intelligence? How did it start? What does it encompass?

Starting from scratch sounds daunting, but it offers a clean slate with no preconceived notions. In a sense, you are learning just as a child might, and making the connections that a child would. In his book, *How to Write With the Skill of a Master and the Genius of a Child*, Marshall J. Cook suggests that you be absolutely open about your ignorance. "The only dumb question is the one you didn't ask because you were too shy, or too concerned about maintaining an aura of knowledgeability and intelligence to ask." He also suggests that writers follow the example of Peter Falk's iconic TV detective, Columbo, who asked endless

> You are learning just as a child might, and making the connections that a child would.

questions but always came back with, "There's just one thing I don't understand."

Most nonfiction writers we talked to said that they first read all the children's books that have already been written on the subject. They do not take notes, but they learn what the competition is. How did other writers approach the subject? How old is the information? Are the books for the same age level you plan to write for? What gaps exist in the information?

When Peggy began her artificial intelligence project, she learned that most children's books on this subject focused on robotics because this angle captures the imagination and offers interesting photo possibilities. She also noticed there was a gap in the information, with very little written about ways in which artificial intelligence might be used in homes, for example, in computer games, coffeemakers, and other appliances that kids are familiar with. She knew this angle would play heavily in her own approach to artificial intelligence.

Some people have the idea that the information in a children's book is somehow less important, less accurate, and less rigorously researched than information in other types of books. That notion couldn't be further from the truth.

Some people have the idea that the information in a children's book is somehow less important, less accurate, and less rigorously researched than information in other types of books. That notion couldn't be further from the truth. Children's writers feel a great responsibility to get the facts straight. Our book might be the only one a child reads on a subject, and that material may be remembered for a long time. Erroneous information is the culprit behind the mistaken belief held by many adults that porcupines shoot their quills, and that the number of spots on a ladybug's back tells how old it is.

Researching children's nonfiction requires much more than reading children's books and encyclopedia articles on the topic. "It is important to know that a writer has really done their homework," says Randi Rivers, editor at Charlesbridge Publishing. She prefers to see a bibliography that is balanced with a variety of primary and secondary source materials.

Secondary Sources

Biographer Nancy Whitelaw dives into her research by reading as much adult material that pertains to her subject as she can find. "I just start reading," she says. "I like thick books with good bibliographies that show me where the authors found their information." Like markers on a hiking trail, a bibliography can lead you through the forest of information. Many of the books and articles listed will be secondary sources whose authors were not experts in the field, nor did they personally experience the event. But the writers have synthesized the material and put it into some kind of perspective as it relates to other events. Secondary sources corroborate facts, and provide a strong foundation on which to build your research.

As you read, be mindful that these books were written through the eyes of a writer, like yourself, who has a bias and opinion, which may or may not reflect your point of view. Give yourself a wide spectrum of materials to select from. Be critical. How is the material presented? Does the author support his argument? Is the data accurate? What is the author's background? Books written by experts in the field are more reliable and should figure high on your list. Who published the book or article? University presses and magazines like the *Smithsonian* or *National Geographic* that are affiliated with research organizations are usually trustworthy.

While most editors prefer to see recently published titles on your bibliography because they have the most up-to-date information, don't neglect older titles. Older nonfiction books often provide more detailed historical elements, and highlight the early years of a product's development—details that may be glossed over in more recent titles. They may also provide just the right anecdote you are looking for.

File-by-the-Pile vs. Neat 'n Tidy

We asked a number of non-fiction writers how they keep their research organized. We learned that it is best to find what works for you and stick with it.

Roxane Chadwick (author of *Amelia Earhart: Aviation Pioneer*) fills notebooks with photocopies and notes taken by hand. "I usually divide the notebook into sections, i.e. setting, history, tidbits, or time periods. My first draft is heavily footnoted using a key to my bibliography of resources. . . . . As my drafts progress, I lose the footnotes."

Carol Johmann (author of *The Lewis & Clark Expedition*) doesn't trust notes. "I like photocopies. I've also trained myself to listen well and retain much of what I hear and read in my head."

Joanne Mattern (author of *The Big Book of the Civil War: Fascinating Facts about the Civil War, Including Historic Photographs, Maps, and Documents*) makes a pile for each project she's working on. "Then, as I work on a project, I sort the piles by topic or relevance. It's messy, but it works for me."

Nancy Butts (author of *Nature's Numbers*) favors computer software designed for writers. It makes her notes easily searchable, and gives her the ability to supplement written notes with relevant audio and video files. She uses the software's "virtual index cards" to plot out her stories, shuffling and reshuffling to her heart's content.

Brandon Marie Miller (author of *George Washington for Kids: His Life and Times*) writes information on index cards.

Jim Murphy (author of *An American Plague*) takes notes in spiral notebooks, collects newspaper and magazine articles, purchases numerous books, and sticks loads of post-its in all of them. "I collect all of these things in large plastic containers and have them stacked in my little office."

Primary Sources

When I decided to write about spiders, I knew there were lots of spider books for children, so I had to find a way for mine to be a bit different. As I began to read about the amazing process of spinning the silk and the different patterns of webs, I knew that spider webs would be my focus. Our oldest son and his wife found an amazing old book in a used bookstore that gave me just what I needed. The author, Winifred Duncan, was so curious about spider webs that she spent a summer and fall on Cape Cod watching a variety of spiders at work in her garden and in every corner of her house. Her book, *Webs in the Wind*, published in 1949, is illustrated with her careful drawings of every kind of web she could find. As I read her descriptions of the spiders spinning their webs in the instinctive patterns of their species, I felt as though I'd been there watching, too. Because Duncan's book recounts her personal experience with spiders it is called a primary source. The person who conducted the research or experienced the event wrote it.

> As often as you can, it is best to find and rely on primary sources.

As often as you can, it is best to find and rely on primary sources. They offer the most accurate information, and provide authentic details of a time period, an event, or a person that a secondary source might not include. More and more, book and magazine editors are requiring their authors to feature primary sources in their work.

Diaries, journals, personal letters, ship logs, company accounts, government documents, research papers, and academic journal articles are all primary sources. Be creative. When Jim Giblin wrote *Chimney Sweeps* he tracked down Parliamentary investigation reports involving child labor and the living conditions of young British chimney sweeps. Peggy read actual case files of the Erie County forensic anthropologist for *Talking Bones*, and Louise Borden, author of *The Journey That Saved Curious George*, sifted through letters, notebooks, photographs, and expense records of Margret and H. A. Rey that she tracked down in the de Grummond Children's Literature Collection at the University of Southern Mississippi.

Jim Murphy's award-winning history books are known for their riveting firsthand accounts of war, weather, and plagues. "I'm always searching for quotes," he says, "that sound as if the individual is talking to us in their front parlor—lively, informed, sometimes humorous, sometimes annoyed. The voice, in other words, of a real person and not someone writing in stilted formal language." To find those primary sources he lurks in libraries, bookstores, historical societies, and museums across the country.

> "I'm always searching for quotes that sound as if the individual is talking to us in their front parlor—lively, informed, sometimes humorous, sometimes annoyed."

While flipping through a book of pension applications by Revolutionary War veterans from 1832, Murphy realized that the applicants had to have been fairly young back in 1775. "I took down the names of all of the soldiers who were 18 or younger when they served and then went searching for more information about each one." A few weeks later he found a copy of Joseph Plumb Martin's recollections in a museum in Morristown, New Jersey. This information became the basis for his book, *A Young Patriot*.

Murphy acknowledges that sheer luck can play a role in locating primary sources. Browsing in a used bookstore he found a copy of a book published just one month after the 1871 fire that destroyed much of Chicago. "I discovered that it was mostly a very dry listing of the buildings destroyed and their value, but tucked in the middle were two long sections entitled 'Personal Recollections.' I plucked two or three of the best from here, then went to Chicago and visited the Chicago Historical Society to dig out more."

Where to Dig

You may not know exactly what you are looking for, but you should know where to look or at least where to start your search. There is a universe of information at your fingertips with just a click of the mouse, and while the computer is a great place to start digging for general information, it is even more useful as a research-planning tool. Use it to locate libraries holding in-depth books on your topic, organizations that have relevant primary source collections, and experts who might give interviews. With a little legwork you can learn to navigate through the specific resources in your area, starting, of course, with your local library.

Public Libraries

Most nonfiction writers, as well as fiction writers, rely on their local librarians to guide them to the best sources available. Become familiar with your library's computer catalog so you can retrieve exactly what you want. Besides what you see on the shelves, every library has a cache of literary gems hidden away that you may have to ask for—like local history information, bound period newspapers, or items still in outdated modes of technology like microfiche or microfilm.

No matter how small your library is, it probably provides access to many other library collections. Find out exactly how far your librarian's arm can reach.

In addition to books, most libraries subscribe to online databases that index hundreds of magazines and journals. Databases such as InfoTrac, LexisNexis, MasterFILE, and ProQuest even contain full-text articles that you can print out. There are databases that cover business topics, medicine, genealogy, arts, science, and current events. Ask your local librarian to show you the different databases and what they offer.

No matter how small your library is, it probably provides access to many other library collections through interlibrary loan. You can usually search catalogs to check the availability of material, and request it from your home computer. If a rare edition that you want to quote is not available through the usual inter-library loan channels, you may need a librarian's assistance. Librarians can often request material outside their jurisdiction from college libraries, out-of-state collections, or museums. Find out exactly how far your librarian's arm can reach. One writer found that a title she was seeking about the Amish was not in any public library. She did, however, locate it at the college library at Colgate University, and with the help of her local librarian, she had the title within a week. If the material cannot be circulated, ask if pertinent sections can be photocopied for you.

Nonfiction writer Carol Johmann's experiences confirm that, "No matter how good you are at doing research, there's always an expert who knows more." For her title *Going West*, the story hinged on a fictional family in 1852 heading west via the Erie Canal, a steamboat across Lake Erie, and a train to Cincinnati. Johmann's local library confirmed that steamboats crisscrossed Erie at that time, and a couple of phone calls confirmed the traffic on the Erie Canal. But did a rail line from the southern shore of Lake Erie to Cincinnati exist in 1852?

The local library couldn't help, nor could the university library, the New York Museum of Transportation, and several railroad companies. "At wits' end, I called the Cincinnati Public Library and asked my question of the reference librarian. In less than two minutes, she had a reference book in front of her that had a dated map showing the route I needed to exist," says Johmann. "The construct of our book was saved."

The Library of Congress

The largest United States public library, the Library of Congress in Washington, D.C., is also the largest library in the world. It holds millions of books, recordings, manuscripts, maps, and photographs, some of which have been digitized and made available online. The library maintains more than 200 databases with abstracts, indexes, and full text documents as well as links to other collections from across the globe. One of our favorite resources through the Library of Congress is the American Folklife Center, where you can listen to excerpts from the StoryCorps Project, hear former slaves telling their stories in the Voices From the Days of Slavery collection, and peruse the numerous personal accounts of U.S. veterans as part of the Veterans History Project. Access it all through www.loc.gov.

College Libraries

If you are writing about science, medicine, or another topic that would require the use of academic journals you most likely will need to go to a college library. Most public libraries do not carry these expensive subscriptions. You can usually access a college catalog online and use the materials on-site, but you will not be able to request material or check it out unless you are a student or alumni. Call ahead to find out what the requirements are. A nominal alumni fee may be a wise investment for easy access to the material. Otherwise, plan on making lots of photocopies or reading the material on the premises.

Museums and Historical Societies

Even the smallest village historical society contains a wealth of information, the most important being primary source documents like diaries, letters, business records, government proceedings, period newspapers, and town meeting minutes. The material may not be cataloged so prepare to browse or pick the brain of the town historian for information. State historical societies may have more of their documents cataloged and digitized online. The Ohio Historical Society, for example, has more than one thousand historic markers photographed and documented on its website (www.ohiohistory.org).

Through the Internet, you can search museum library holdings like the Museum of Modern Art Library (www.moma.org/learn/resources/library), which has 300,000 books, 300 periodical subscriptions, and more than 40,000 vertical files of information about artists and their work. The collection is non-circulating but material can be requested through interlibrary loan or used on-site. The American Museum of Natural History website (www.amnh.org) offers access to hundreds of free electronic journals like *Advances in Astronomy*, *Dental Anthropology Newsletter*, and the *Zoological Journal of the Linnean Society.* The Smithsonian Institution in Washington, D.C. (www.si.edu) provides links to 16 museums and 1.2 million volumes. And the library at the United States Holocaust Memorial Museum (www.ushmm.org) holds more than 85,000 items, many of which are primary source documents.

Locate specialty museums and ask for their assistance. If you are writing about baseball, for instance, contact the National Baseball Hall of Fame and Museum in Cooperstown. Need to know about the first women cyclists? Call the Pedaling History Bicycle Museum in Orchard Park, New York. There are hundreds of museums dedicated to everything from aluminum Christmas trees to footwear. When you go, take copious notes. Accurately record bibliographic information right down to the drawer number where the item was located just in case you have to make a return trip.

> There are hundreds of museums dedicated to everything from aluminum Christmas trees to footwear.

Catching Information with the Net

Sitting in front of your computer, you are faced with a virtual library that is exponentially larger than the contents of the Library of Congress. According to WorldWideWebSize.com, a site that monitors online growth, there are more than 14 billion pages on the indexed Web. An Internet search sifts through only a fraction of that information, yet it is still more than enough for you to find the facts you need.

With all that data floating around on the Internet you must develop the skill to evaluate what you find. Excellent expert sources will be listed alongside dubious ones written by third-grade students or by people with an axe to grind. There are clues, though, that can help you assess the validity and/or accuracy of any Web page.

The Museum of *What*?

There are hundreds of quirky museums with specialists who are more than eager to help you find the information you need. Here are just a few offbeat subjects and places you can find unusual facts about them:

Fish: Fresh Water Fishing Hall of Fame, 10360 Hall of Fame Drive, Hayward, WI 54843. (715) 634-4440. www.freshwater-fishing.org

Illegal drugs: Drug Enforcement Administration Museum. 700 Army Navy Drive, Arlington, VA 22202. (202) 307-3463. www.deamuseum.org

Jell-O: Jell-O Gallery, 23 E. Main St, Le Roy, NY 14482. (585) 768-7433. www.jellogallery.org

LEGO toys: Toy & Plastic Brick Museum, 4597 Noble Street, Bellaire, OH 43906. (740) 671-8890. www.danstoymuseum.blogspot.com

Mustard: National Mustard Museum, 7477 Hubbard Ave., Middleton, WI 53562. (800) 438-6878. www.mustardmuseum.com

PEZ: Burlingame Museum of PEZ Memorabilia, 214 California Drive, Burlingame, CA 94010. (650) 347-2301. www.burlingamepezmuseum.com

Shoes: Bata Shoe Museum, 327 Bloor St. West, Toronto, Ontario M5S 1W7 Canada. (416) 979-7799. www.batashoemuseum.ca

Teeth: Dr. Samuel D. Harris National Museum of Dentistry at the University of Maryland, 31 South Greene St., Baltimore, MD 21201-1504. (410) 706-0600. www.dentalmuseum.org

Toilets: Plumbing Museum, 80 Rosedale Rd., Watertown, MA 02471. (617) 926-2111. http://theplumbingmuseum.org

Who wrote the information? Look for an author's name. Is it a writer you recognize from other authoritative works, or a tech-savvy seventh grader who posted his book report?

Who established the website? Look at the header or footer for the site's affiliation, or the name of the organization that is responsible for its content. Reputable organizations usually have a screening process to make sure documents meet their standards. Often, the articles are peer reviewed. Is the site run by a legitimate organization that is recognized in the field you are researching or is it posted by an individual with no known authority?

Look at the URL (the Internet address of the document) and the domain name, which is the text name corresponding to that address. For example, the URL *http://www.Peggythomaswrites.com* contains the domain name of Peggythomaswrites. The domain type is *.com*. Commercial sites carry a .com suffix and generally have a bias toward promoting their information, product, or service. Government sites, listed as *.gov*, are sponsored by the United States government. Government organizations such as the U.S. Geological Survey, the Department of Transportation, the Department of the Treasury, and the White House all have .gov websites. Military sites, however, are listed as *.mil*. The suffix *.org* refers to organizations including museums, religious groups, charities, and lobbying organizations. Universities and schools of higher learning are listed with *.edu*. As a general rule of thumb, government, educational sites, and organizations contain more reliable information than commercial sites. But choose the websites that suit your purpose. For example, military sites are a good place to get current recruitment numbers and information straight from the Pentagon, but they won't be the best place to look for an unbiased opinion of a military operation or where to find a peace rally.

Check out other sites that are linked to the website you are viewing, which may provide a clue to the bias. Although information is rarely neutral, some data can be interpreted in different ways depending on the author's intentions. Is an account of the Holocaust linked to a Neo-Nazi group, or the Jewish League? A less obvious example would be product information obtained from a manufacturer's website. It may be accurate, but chances are it will give a more favorable view of the product's quality and reliability compared to a consumer website.

"When I see a bibliography with lots of websites, that really scares me." Strike a balance and use a wide variety of materials.

Don't assume that an Internet document offers the most current information available. Websites can remain unchanged for years. Reliable sites often list the date the site was last updated, or they have a copyright date. If no date is given, you may be able to view the website's directory, accessed at the bottom of the site, for the latest modification.

Select your Internet sources carefully. Even if you find reputable current websites, use them sparingly. "When I see a bibliography with lots of websites," says editor Randi Rivers, "that really scares me." Strike a balance and use a wide variety of materials.

There are Internet information databases that you can log on to for free with your library card via your local library or, for a fee, you can subscribe to sites like HighBeam.com or NewspaperArchive.com in order to access full texts of many scholarly journals, newspapers, and magazines. However, there are databases you can use for free without going through your library. EBSCO, which many libraries subscribe to, offers a free version at www.ebscohost.com. The Education Resources Information Center (www.eric.ed.gov) and Science.gov are sponsored by the United States government, and Googlescholar.com is a growing searchable database for academic papers and studies.

Useful Reference Websites

Dictionary: Dictionary.com at http://dictionary.reference.com/
Includes several dictionaries, a thesaurus, and encyclopedias.

General Reference: Ref Desk.com at www.refdesk.com/
Offers a quote, article, and website of the day as well as a feature called "This Day in History," with links to almost everything.

Geography: CIA's World Factbook at https://www.cia.gov/library/publications/the-world-factbook/index.html
Get up-to-date information about any country in the world, including its culture, currency, flag, population, products, and more.

History: Historical Census Browser at http://fisher.lib.virginia.edu/collections/stats/histcensus/index.html
Provides information about the ethnicity, education, and population of states and counties, as collected by the U.S. Census Bureau from 1790 to 1960.

Holidays: Holidays on the Net at www.holidays.net
Find out what people are celebrating each day of the year.

Quotations: Bartleby at www.bartleby.com
Find or verify a quotation from thousands of sources, searching by author or subject.

Time: Time and Date.com at www.timeanddate.com
Contains the World Clock, time zones, a distance calculator, a sunrise and sunset calculator, and date calculators.

Translations: Babel Fish at http://babelfish.yahoo.com
Type in a word or phrase and translate it to or from English, Chinese, Dutch, Greek, Italian, and more.

Something Old, Something New

When you choose a subject that's been written about many times, you have to give it something new. When I was writing *Lizards Weird and Wonderful*, my goal was to include at least one new piece of information about lizards that I didn't know before, and that readers might not know either. It was a challenge, but it was fun. For example, I knew that if you try to catch a small lizard by the tail, you're likely to find yourself holding the tail while the lizard runs away and grows a new one. But I didn't know how a lizard could make its tail separate so easily, and even more amazing, what gave it the ability to regenerate.

I had been reading books on reptiles written by college professors and herpetologists, so I called one of these specialists. I don't think many people asked him for that information, because he seemed very happy to explain how lizards can make their tail drop off and grow a new one. And I had something new for a well-worn topic.

Newspapers, journals, and magazines such as the *New York Times*, *Smithsonian*, *Natural History*, and *National Geographic* often mention the names of scientists doing new research that may not have been discussed in a children's book before. My lizard book got another boost when, after much research, I found a small article in a nature magazine about the "Gecko Team," a group of scientists that discovered how a gecko can walk upside down on a ceiling thanks to specialized structures on its feet. And I quoted the last paragraph from the same article: "The Gecko Team's discovery could lead to inventions such as stronger adhesive tape that can be used many times, or gecko tape for attaching equipment to space stations. And imagine gecko gloves and shoes that would let rock climbers or robots move around like Spider Man."

In a *National Geographic* article I discovered scientists who studied the wetapunga, an insect from New Zealand that was new to me and likely to be new to most readers of *The Big Bug Book*. And in another article I found the name of a scientist in Hawaii who discovered the "green grappler," the first carnivorous caterpillar ever known. I was the first writer to describe it in a children's book.

Photo Research

Another element to your research may be locating photographs to use with your story. Magazine editors appreciate authors who can provide photographs or at least guide them to the appropriate sources, and some book contracts require the author to supply photographs as well as text.

Start your search for photos right away. The minute author Carla Killough McClafferty begins her subject research she is also looking for photographs to use in her book. "Keep track of where the images are housed and any copyright information you can find," McClafferty advises. "It is easier to do [photo research] as you go, rather than backtrack later." Ann Bausum, author of *Freedom Riders*, agrees. "Be a stickler for organization so that you don't lose track of image sources, dates taken, identities of image contact, etc. You'll need all of that information in order to write photo captions and to verify your rights to use an illustration."

Depending on the subject matter, your search for photos will take you to many different places, but here are two sources to start with:

- **Interviewees.** You will probably locate the best photos from the people you have personally interviewed. Ask if photos are available and if you can see them.

- **Government sources.** As a U.S. citizen, you are entitled to use photographs from government agencies. One of the best resources, especially for historical subjects, is the Prints and Photographs Reading Room at the Library of Congress (www.loc.gov/pictures/). About 75 percent of the collection is described online, but the best way to access the photos is to go to Washington, D.C. and select them yourself. Contact NASA for space photographs; the U.S. Geological Survey for pictures of volcanoes, hurricanes, and other natural phenomena; and the Smithsonian Institution for photos pertaining to natural history, history, art, and culture.

By the time you have written the first or second draft, you should have a good idea of the kinds of photos you'll need. Bausum says she turns reference images over to her publisher when the project goes to design, providing multiple options for the art director to choose from. Near the end of the editorial process, when it is clear which images will be used, she acquires the permissions.

Like text, photographs are copyrighted. Many of the photos at the Library of Congress are in the public domain, which means no copyright exists, but it is the author's responsibility to obtain permission if an image is protected. This can sometimes be tricky. For her book, *In Defiance of Hitler: The Secret Mission of Varian Fry*, McClafferty wanted to use several images housed at the Museum of Modern Art, only to discover that MoMA didn't own the rights. The photographer had died in 1955, leaving an unknown heir in control. McClafferty followed the trail to the Center for Creative Photography in Arizona where she received the heir's old email address. "I frantically emailed this man—hoping and praying the address was still good." It was, and he graciously granted McClafferty permission to use the photographs in her award-winning book.

> By the time you have written the first or second draft, you should have a good idea of the kinds of photos you'll need.

Searching for photos can lead to pleasant surprises too. Bausum recalls tracking down suffrage leader Elizabeth Cady Stanton's great-great-granddaughter for photographs. "My Stanton family contact introduced me to her mother," says Bausum, "a veteran of the closing years of the woman suffrage campaign, and this spry octogenarian entertained me with reminiscences from a fight that involved three generations of her family."

Photo Research Sources

Picture research can be time-consuming, but it helps if you start with some idea of where to look. Here is a select list of photo sources, most of which offer searchable image banks and a variety of subject areas.

Corbis: 710 Second Avenue, Suite 200, Seattle, WA 98104. (206) 373-6000. www.corbisimages.com

The Official Museum Directory: American Association of Museums, 1575 Eye Street NW, Suite 400, Washington, D.C. 20005. (202) 289-1818. www.aam-us.org

Picture History: www.picturehistory.com

Smithsonian Photographic Services: 600 Maryland Ave., SW, Washington, D.C. 20013. http://photo2.si.edu

Stockphotorequest.com: P.O. Box 341, Flagstaff, AZ 86002. (928) 214-8272. www.stockphotorequest.com

United States National Archives & Records Administration: 8601 Adelphi Road, College Park, MD 20740-6001. (866) 272-6272. www.archives.gov

Before submitting any photos, review the submission policy of your publisher. Sometimes writers start by sending photocopies or low-resolution scans of proposed images for the publisher to comment on and critique, then the final selections are submitted as high-quality digital images, prints, or slides. (Book publishers typically prefer to work with digital files, while some magazines still accept prints and slides.) Digital images should be no less than 300 dpi, but check with your editor first.

Fact Checking

We won't lie to you. Sometimes we feel a great sense of anxiety about writing nonfiction. Although fiction writers get letters from frantic readers moaning, "How could you *do* that to my favorite character?" no one can say they are wrong. Nonfiction writers, on the other hand, can be wrong. We can make all sorts of mistakes. We might misinform the reader, misquote an expert, misrepresent a source, or misspell someone's name. The number of things that can go wrong is mystifying. The only way to overcome this unsettling panic is to double, triple, and quadruple check your facts and have confidence in your interpretation of those facts.

Data such as the name of the gold medal-winning hockey team of 2006 or the date of the Reformation may be corroborated with many written sources. But other bits of information may not be so easy to verify. While writing a biography of mathematician Grace Hopper, Peggy wanted to use an anecdote about how Hopper wheeled her top-secret papers around the Pentagon using a little red wagon. Peggy could not verify the anecdote, though, so she had a choice to either include it with a caveat or throw it away. Because none of her primary sources, or her most reliable secondary sources, ever mentioned the wagon, she did not use it. But if the source that mentioned the wagon had been a reliable one, she might have used the anecdote and simply said, "One source said that . . ." or "It was rumored that she dragged her papers around in a wagon." If you choose to include unverifiable information you might be undermining your credibility.

Verify information using your secondary source material, and ultimately your primary sources. Keep a detailed list of the people, places, and organizations that you've read about.

Navigating through print and electronic materials is the first step to doing thorough research, but there's more to it. Get even closer to your topic by meeting the people you want to write about and visiting the places you will be describing. There is nothing better than hands-on research and live interviews to give your writing fresh material and a new perspective.

Building a Bibliography

It will save time if you record all your sources in bibliographic form when you take notes. *The Chicago Manual of Style* shows how to cite just about any kind of source; there are also many online tools that can generate citations in just about every style. Here are some sample entries for the most common research sources:

Books

Zinsser, William. *On Writing Well: The Classic Guide to Writing Nonfiction, Seventh Edition—revised and updated*. NY: Harper Perennial, 2006. (If no author is given, list book alphabetically by title.)

Magazines

Aronson, Marc. "Originality in Nonfiction." *School Library Journal*, January 2006. Volume 1, issue 1, p. 42-43.

Internet Articles

Backes, Laura. 2009. "Finding Your Voice." *Children's Book Insider* www.write4kids.com/feature3.html (accessed June 4, 2010).

Journal Articles from a Database

Swindoll, Barry. 2008. "Writer's Eye Strain." *British Medical Journal* 320: 123+. ProQuest. http://il.proquest.com (accessed May 31, 2009).

Interviews

Rivers, Randi, Editor at Charlesbridge, phone interview, 10:00am, September 19, 2006. (If the interview was done in person, note the location also.)

Emails

Bowman-Kruhm, Mary, email message to author, June 4, 2010.

Chapter 4
Talking Bones
Research Part II

In-person Interviews

Phone/Email Interviews

Hands-on Research

Quoting

"Breathe the air, witness the light, and settle in the place of your words."
—Carolyn Yoder, author and editor

Editor Carolyn Yoder says, "Writing nonfiction or historical fiction—any writing that involves research—should not be lonely, dusty work." That is easy to forget when you are elbow deep in an archival file box, but it is true. All around you are fascinating, knowledgeable people—some of whom may know a great deal about your subject. If you take the time to ask, you may be rewarded with a lively and revealing conversation that brings new ideas to the forefront.

As Yoder puts it, "People should be a big part of research." This means conducting interviews and experiencing the world around you so that you can give your writing color, a distinct voice, and the authority it needs. It's easy to take your research to this next level, and it can be lots of fun. Let's start with the art of the interview.

Interviews

Interviewing an expert or someone with personal experience on your topic is a great way to verify the facts that you have gathered from books, journals, and the Internet. Some information, like statistics, may be out-dated before the book or article is even printed, and events that are ongoing change from minute to minute. A specialist can keep you current and give you insight into what it all means.

A dynamite quote gleaned from an interview adds a voice other than your own to the story, which can be important when you are not the expert. Why should a reader take your article seriously? Quoting the chief of pediatrics about head injuries, for example, lets readers know you took the time to research bike helmets and they can trust what you have to report.

> A dynamite quote gleaned from an interview adds a voice other than your own to the story.

Interviews also add what a reporter would call "color." Meeting a person in their natural habitat gives you the small details that you would miss otherwise. Note a person's facial expression, body language, and cadence of speech. Is the mother of quintuplets frazzled? Does she unknowingly have a lollipop stuck in her hair or is she composed and calmly pouring coffee into china cups? Does the math professor's office look like a lesson in geometry or chaos theory? These details observed during an interview help you recreate the setting for your reader, and bring your subject to life.

Facklam Files:

The Color of Urgency: Peggy's Observations at the New England Aquarium

Once I conducted an interview with the general curator and director of animal husbandry at the New England Aquarium. I was ushered through security doors and into the hospital area, where they nurse sick fish and marine mammals from aquarium exhibits, and rehabilitate wild animals that have been stranded on the beach or rescued from fishing nets. One thing that struck me as we entered the brightly lit hallway was the pan of disinfectant at the door. Anyone who entered had to step into the pan and over to the other side in an awkward dance to ensure that no germs were tracked in. *We don't even do that at the hospital ICU,* I thought. But here, members of some of the most endangered species cling to life.

Transport kennels for seals and stretchers for whales and dolphins of all sizes lined the narrow hallway in easy reach. The computerized emergency monitoring system blinked and whirred quietly in the cramped office that was jammed with other emergency supplies. This was clearly a place designed for rapid response.

At one tank, a team of biologists and volunteers trained recovering harbor seals to eat live fish again after being weaned off of seafood milkshakes. One straggly pup was not getting the hang of it. I watched while the vet straddled the seal and pushed a fish down its gullet. The rest of the team looked on in silence, their brows furrowed in concern, knowing that the seal would not be returned to the ocean if it could not hunt live prey.

When I went home and wrote the chapter "Stranded Seals and Beached Babies" for *Marine Mammal Preservation*, I felt confident that I could describe the hospital area in detail so my readers would understand the urgency and gravity of the work being done at the aquarium.

Finding Someone to Interview

How do you find experts in the first place? Keep a list of all the people mentioned in the books and articles you have read so far. You already know that they are open to being interviewed, and they may be willing to talk to you as well. But be careful of overexposure. You may not want the same voices that have already had a chance to speak on the subject. Or you may want a second or third opinion.

Check out the organizations that are referred to in your reading. If more than two people have an interest in a subject, then there is likely to be an association, organization, or government agency promoting it. When Peggy was writing her series, the Science of Saving Animals, she contacted the American Zoo and Aquarium Association, World Wildlife Fund, National Wildlife Federation, National Audubon Society, NASA, National Oceanic and Atmospheric Administration, North American Bluebird Society, New York State Department of Environmental Conservation, the U.S. Fish and Wildlife Service, and the U.S. Army Corps of Engineers, just to name a few. Each group provided her with names of people she could talk to.

> If more than two people have an interest in a subject, then there is likely to be an association, organization, or government agency promoting it.

To locate appropriate organizations, try one of several website directories. ProfNet (https://profnet.prnewswire.com) maintains a list of "professional communicators" from a variety of businesses, organizations, and agencies; and Newswise Contact Directory (www.newswise.com/resources/ncd) allows you to select contacts by subject, everything from agoraphobia to zoology. Both sites were designed to help journalists and nonfiction writers connect with people who are happy to talk about their chosen field.

Another way to find professionals is through a college or university public relations office. When I was writing *The Big Bug Book*, I needed information about giant insects. Cornell University is half a day's drive from our town, and I knew the school had a huge insect collection. So I called the public relations office, described the book I was writing, and asked if they could direct me to someone in the entomology department who might be willing to talk to me. The PR director was happy to do that, and my son, Paul, who illustrated the book, came along for the interview. The professor even gave Paul a live, giant Madagascar hissing cockroach, which later lived on Paul's art table in its own Tupperware house.

My husband and I used this approach for our climate book, too. Through the PR department we learned that the University of Buffalo houses one of the world's collections of ice cores, which are drilled out of glaciers so they can be studied for signs of climate change. Most museums, businesses, medical centers, and research institutes have a publicity department or a public relations office that would be happy to connect you with the right person.

Every day people log on to the Web and cruise through professional and recreational message boards and listservs, often responding to queries posted by people like us. For this book, we posted questions in the Yahoo! Group NF FOR KIDS (http://groups.yahoo.com/group/NFforKids) to take the pulse of what nonfiction writers thought about story in nonfiction, how they got ideas, and their opinions about online critique groups.

You may want to be an observer for a few days before posting a query, to get a feel for what kinds of questions are being asked and who the participants are. Before you submit your post, clearly state who you are and that you are doing research for a book or magazine project. Although many message boards have a privacy clause, you might find someone who will agree to a phone interview or email you directly.

Your family comes in handy, too, sometimes. One son's alumni magazine from Ohio State led me to Dr. Sally Boysen's Primate Cognition

Center, where I met the chimpanzees who count. When my husband and I were writing a book called *Healing Drugs*, two of our sons—who are both in pharmacology research—described the long process of getting a new drug through the rigors of FDA approval. They also vetted the book for us.

The Expert Next Door

There is a saying that an expert is someone who lives more than 100 miles away. This is a myth we would like to dispel. It may be hard to believe that a guy who lives a couple of blocks away is an expert on toxic toads or a professional ballroom dancer, but it happens.

> It may be hard to believe that a guy who lives a couple of blocks away is an expert on toxic toads or a professional ballroom dancer, but it happens.

Amazing people live everywhere, even in your hometown. Where we live outside of Buffalo, New York, we are proud to have had Wilson Greatbatch, who invented the pacemaker; Bill Tolhurst, a world-renowned trainer of scent dogs for the police; and Belva Lockwood, one of the first women to run for president, just to name a few.

As a writer with two young children and a part-time job, Peggy found it hard to make long trips to conduct personal interviews. But what she could do was drive a short distance for the same information. While working on *Big Cat Conservation*, she needed to talk to people who worked with lions, tigers, and leopards, three animals that are hard to come by in rural Western New York. So she called the Buffalo Zoo and was treated to a behind-the-scenes look in the big cat house. She met Boris the Siberian tiger, and learned that the Buffalo Zoo was on the cutting edge of conservation: It keeps the Species Survival Plan for every captive clouded leopard in the world. If a zoo in Portugal wants to breed a clouded leopard, for example, it would have to contact the Buffalo Zoo first. She got expert advice on big cat breeding right in her own backyard.

Every spring we visit the Iroquois National Wildlife Refuge and watch a pair of bald eagles nesting in a 70-foot basswood tree. It is bird watching at its high-tech best, sitting in the nature center looking at a live video feed on television. Today, dozens of cameras are focused on nests and burrows and can be viewed on the Internet, but little did we realize that the Iroquois refuge was the first to do this. So Peggy interviewed their naturalist for her book *Bird Alert* as well as for a feature article in the *Buffalo News*.

Take a moment to think about where you live. Who could you shine a light on in an article, or interview for a book? What famous or infamous events have taken place within an hour's drive of your home? Brag about the people, places, and events in your hometown.

Setting Up an Interview

Planning ahead is key to getting the best outcome from an interview. Prepare yourself as well as the interviewee so that both of you know what to expect. Here's how:

- **Call first.** Nobody likes to have unexpected visitors, so call first and ask permission for an interview. The phone is the quickest way to make contact, but some writers like Fred Bortz, author of *Astrobiology*, prefer mailing a letter while others zip off an email to their prospective interviewees.

- **Don't be shy.** In your email, phone call, or letter, clearly state your name and your intentions. Mention the name of the magazine or book publisher that you are contracted with, or if an editor has expressed interest in the piece.

- **Be accommodating.** Make the interview as convenient for the interviewee as possible. Work around his or her schedule, not yours. Be aware of time differences if calling across the country. Avoid mealtimes, early morning hours, and late at night. Be flexible, and let your interviewee choose the time.

- **Do your homework.** Before an interview, learn as much as you can about the person and the subject so you have a base of knowledge to start with. If your interviewee has written a book or academic journal article, read it. You don't want to waste time having the person explain basic information that you should already know. However, if you don't understand something you have read, this is the perfect opportunity to ask for clarification. Blame it on your young readers; they need it simplified.

- **Start early.** Don't leave expert interviews until a week before your deadline. You might know a lot about the subject, but you may run out of time. People are busy and are often hard to track down. It may take more than one attempt to set up the interview, so give yourself plenty of lead time, especially if you want the person to read and comment on the transcript or pertinent parts of the manuscript.

- **Suggest a time frame.** Schedule the appropriate amount of time for the interview to take place, usually no more than an hour. It is very disheartening to drive a long distance to interview someone, or arrange for an uninterrupted phone call, only to find that after 10 minutes he or she needs to make a hasty exit.

Isabel Wilkerson, a Pulitzer Prize-winning journalist, calls an interview a "guided conversation." For her the overall experience is more important than the actual questions.

Conducting an Interview

Doing a person-to-person interview can be intimidating, especially for someone who has never conducted an interview before, or is not very outgoing. It is a multi-tasking activity. You ask questions, listen to answers, jot down key points, observe your surroundings, and think ahead to new questions all at the same time. But ditch the notebook and all you really have is a conversation with a knowledgeable acquaintance.

Isabel Wilkerson, a Pulitzer Prize-winning journalist, calls an interview a "guided conversation." For her the overall experience is more important than the actual questions. "I try to make the interaction as enjoyable as possible."

Here are seven ways to make an interview pleasant for both you and your interviewee, and get the information that you need:

- **Make a personal connection.** If you notice a family photo and see that your children are similar in age, mention it. Together you might commiserate for a minute about high tuition bills or finding a reliable babysitter. Finding familiar ground warms the sometimes austere and chilly interview atmosphere, and relaxes everyone.

- **Prepare a list of questions.** What information do you want to learn from this person? Do you need one specific piece of information, or do you want in-depth material about his or her life, loves, and losses? You may already know that you need a comment or quote about helmet safety to plug into that article, but don't stop there. You may find that a lengthier conversation leads you to a fuller article or gives you a new slant.

- **Avoid questions that evoke a yes or no answer.** Instead of asking, "Was it hard to climb Mount Everest?" ask, "What was the most difficult part of the journey?" or "How did it feel to reach the top?" Understanding someone's emotions is just as important as gathering factual information.

- **Ask for details.** If your interview subject mentions a particular piece of equipment that you may not be familiar with, ask for a more detailed description. What is it used for? What sound does it make? Think like a third grader. What would a young person want to know about it?

- **Ask for an example to get a fuller story.** In an interview with forensic anthropologist Kathleen Arries, Peggy learned lots of general information about how to identify a "John Doe." But when she asked for a specific example, Arries opened up a drawer and pulled out a case file that she had worked on. She laid out photographs and described the case in such detail that Peggy featured it in the identification chapter of *Talking Bones: The Science of Forensic Anthropology.*

- **Don't feel glued to your list of questions.** Follow the natural flow of the conversation, and take your cues from your interviewee. If he or she enjoys explaining a process in detail, explore that issue before moving on to your second question, which might be on a completely different topic. If the conversation veers off into uncharted territory, use your list of questions to guide it back on track.

- **Actually listen to the answers.** This advice may seem obvious, but it is easy to get so caught up in writing down every word that you are no longer paying attention to what the person is saying. To avoid this, learn to write key phrases or words that will remind you of that portion of the interview later. If your interviewee mentions specific statistics or says something especially eloquent, pause the interview for a moment so you can write it down clearly, or ask for clarification.

To Record or Not to Record

We prefer to use a pen and paper to jot down information. But it can be difficult to capture quotes accurately, especially when the interviewee is on a roll. A small hand-held recorder comes in handy. Mary Bowman-Kruhm, author of *The Leakeys: A Biography*, says, "I record interviews on my iPhone with the Recorder app although I also jot some main points down longhand. Recording, however, gives me more time to watch the body language and look the person in the eye."

By law you must tell a person if you are taping the conversation. And even if you decide not to use a recorder, explain your method of documenting the interview. Some people are nervous even when they see you write in a notebook. It also will prevent you from making the same mistake Peggy made years ago during an interview with a reptile rehabilitator.

> Explain your method of documenting the interview. Some people are nervous even when they see you write in a notebook.

Peggy had planned on using a tape recorder, but the woman launched into her tour and speech before Peggy could switch it on. The woman always had her head turned aside picking up an iguana or reaching into a snake's cage. She was on a roll, so Peggy barely asked any questions. Peggy wrote furiously using her turned-off tape recorder under her notebook for extra support. An hour into the tour, the rehabilitator noticed the tape recorder and was annoyed that Peggy hadn't told her the conversation was being recorded. It wasn't, of course, but that didn't matter. The relationship that Peggy wanted to foster with this woman took longer to establish because of this embarrassing incident.

In the past, cassette tape recorders gave us a false sense of security. Many writers have lost at least one interview when the tape jammed, the batteries gave out, or they forgot to push PLAY. Today's digital voice recorders are more versatile and make it even easier to transcribe the interview when it's done. Also, many types of mobile phones, iPods, webcams, and various other electronic devices offer the capability to record audio *and* video, potentially adding a whole new dimension to the interview process. But remember, things can go wrong with digital recording devices too, so cover all your bases. Listen carefully, take notes, and always recharge your equipment before each interview.

"Can I Quote You On That?"

You might think you'll get tons of quotes after a 30-minute interview, but you're mistaken. Occasionally a quote will leap out at you right in the middle of an interview and you have to silence your "Yippee!" until you get back to your office. But most of the time you'll have to review the transcript carefully to find out how someone's words can be used effectively.

If you recorded the conversation, you may notice that your Broadway starlet or your expert on safety helmets does not actually speak in complete sentences. You'll hear lots of *um*'s and *ah*'s too. Don't worry. You can salvage those quotes by deleting those *um*'s and *ah*'s, making your expert sound intelligible. What fits between the quotation marks must be accurate word for word, but as the interviewer and author you have the obligation to present your interviewee fairly. That may mean cleaning up broken and ragged sentences if necessary.

Here is a portion of an interview transcribed from a tape:

> *"The coffin text is, well, it is equivalent to a modern-day résumé with references. Look, besides prayers, deceased's name, and, uh uh, list of uh, ancestors, it also tells the person's occupation and um, his uh, good deeds."*

Here is how it appeared in print:

> *"The coffin text is equivalent to a modern-day résumé with references. Besides prayers, the deceased's name, and list of ancestors, it also tells the person's occupation and good deeds."*

A few unimportant words were deleted for the sake of clarity and to present the anthropologist as the intelligent man he is without altering his meaning or intent.

You also must use quotations in the proper context. If, for example, a farmer said, "Boy, she's a big momma, isn't she?" when speaking of his prized sow, you cannot use those words when writing about his wife. Avoid misrepresenting a person's opinions or views.

The best quotes reflect the person's personality and emotions, or present the information in an interesting way. In *What's the Buzz?* readers get a feel for the scientists' excitement for their research with this quote from David Roubik: "Finding how well the bees communicate really shocked us," he said. "They're not just saying that there's some good food out there, so fly around and maybe you'll find it. They're saying how far away, how high up, and in what direction." Another researcher gave me this vivid analogy to describe how bee larva are raised: "It's like having a child and locking it in a bedroom with a supply of food until the child is full grown."

So weed through your notes and transcripts to find just the right quotes, so that your reader hears the voices of the people you interviewed, gets a feel for their character, and learns something new.

Phone Interviews

You won't always be able to conduct every interview in person. It costs money to travel to far-off cities, and your job or family may keep you tethered close to home. Have no fear—phone interviews are a great substitute, and can be just as effective.

When doing phone interviews, it's important to consider how you can minimize distractions. Let your family know that you are going to be on the phone. If you have walk-in neighbors like we do, tape a sign on your door: SHH! I'M CONDUCTING A PHONE INTERVIEW. Farm out your fussy toddlers to a friend, put them down for a nap, or turn their favorite video on. Don't risk losing a valuable quote because you panic at the sight of one of your children peeking into the office with a dire question. Most people will understand if you need to excuse yourself, but it is best for your own peace of mind if you can concentrate and give the interview your full attention.

How you record a phone interview is up to you. While still in your jammies, you can take notes longhand, type them directly into your computer, or record the conversation using one of many telephone recording devices available at tech shops. Again, tell your interviewee that you are taping the interview, and take notes in case the contraption malfunctions.

The one thing you cannot get from a phone interview is a sense of the person's surroundings. If such information is important to you, ask. "Where do you work?" "What is your office like?" Peggy once conducted a series of phone interviews with a forensic anthropologist from Ohio. It was two months after 9/11 and he was responsible for examining the skeletal remains from the site. Every day on the news we saw images of the search and clean up, but Peggy wanted to know what went on behind the scenes where he worked. One area in particular, Fresh Kills landfill, the site where debris was taken, was off limits, but Peggy knew that a lot of work was being done there. After he described his experience in the city morgue, she asked him to describe the Fresh Kills site on Staten Island. He said he hadn't been there, but handed the phone to his wife, also an anthropologist who was working the night shift at the landfill. She described examining bone fragments under floodlights in a MASH tent while giant earthmovers rumbled past just a few yards away. When it rained she stood in puddles that bubbled with methane gas. "It was an eerie, otherworldly place," she said. Peggy felt like she was there, too.

> She described examining bone fragments under floodlights in a MASH tent while giant earthmovers rumbled past. When it rained she stood in puddles that bubbled with methane gas. "It was an eerie, otherworldly place," she said.

The key to getting this kind of material over the phone is to ask open-ended questions that allow the person to talk, and to ask about sensory details. Does it have a smell? What does it feel like?

Email Interviews

For this book, we interviewed other nonfiction writers via email. Often these emails were followed up by phone interviews, but we made the initial contacts through the Internet.

For some professionals, email is the preferred method of communication and often the only practical way of getting their thoughts down on paper. In your introductory email briefly describe the project you are working on and ask if he or she would be willing to answer a few questions for you. In the subject line write "Interview Request" so the person will open the email even though it is from a stranger. When you receive a positive response, phrase your interview questions carefully. You won't be on the other end of the line to rephrase them if anything comes across as confusing or vague. Again, avoid yes or no answers and ask for specific examples.

One benefit to email interviews is that you have the responses in writing, and are assured of quoting accurately. This method also gives people a chance to ponder your questions at their leisure, which can be both a benefit and a disadvantage. On one hand, you are sure to get thoughtful responses; on the other, the carefully crafted answers may lack that spontaneous gut reaction you were looking for. If an email response sparks your interest, don't hesitate to call the interviewee and ask for clarification or further explanation.

The first book I researched completely by email was *What's the Buzz? The Secret Lives of Bees*. The prospect of relying so heavily on email made me nervous because I was a neophyte emailer at the time, but the book required interviews with scientists at the Smithsonian Tropical Research Institute in Panama, and there was no hope of my getting there in person. The publisher's budget had been spent on a previous author, who had been assigned to do the book and later abandoned it, for reasons I never discovered. So I had to ask questions by email.

It was difficult because I couldn't always understand or "see" exactly what these scientists were telling me. By asking about their day and letting them know what my life was like 2,000 miles north, I developed a friendship with these men and women. Soon their tone changed from academic to conversational, and I received wonderful information that my readers and I could understand.

After the Interview

Immediately after an interview, write or type out your notes and fill in any gaps in your note-taking. Peggy sits in her car and fleshes out everything she can remember before a long drive home, and prefers not to talk to anyone until this job is done. "I can be distracted easily," she says. "And if I don't fix this conversation into my memory I'm liable to forget important details."

Remember your mother's advice: Always write thank-you notes.

Jot down what you remember of the room, the person, and your impressions of the meeting. How would you describe the woman or man you just met? If you recorded the conversation, now you can transcribe the tape. This is a time-consuming process if you do it by hand, but some digital recorders can download interviews directly onto your computer. There are also software programs and online services that will transcribe text for you.

And remember your mother's advice: Always write thank-you notes. A brief handwritten note or an email of thanks to the people you interview is polite and keeps the door of communication open. You may also offer him or her the opportunity to review the piece before it goes to your editor.

Carla Killough McClafferty prefers to email phone interview transcripts to interviewees. "They email me back and they either say, 'Yes everything is correct,' or they might say something like, 'If you add the following, it will be correct.' This way, I have a paper trail that they agreed that what I heard was correct." If you do share the finished manuscript, we recommend only sending that portion of the text which is relevant to the interview. If you would like your interviewee to fact-check the entire manuscript, however, make sure you have plenty of time before your deadline.

Hands-On Research

Of the three means of research—bookwork, interviews, and hands-on—the best approach by far is hands-on. It gives your writing insight that only you can provide by experiencing something personally. Author Louise Borden captured the distinction between these methods beautifully in her description of the research she did on Margret and H. A. Rey. Initially Borden steeped herself in a world of handwritten letters, newsreels, and photos of the 1930s and was later startled by the brilliant color of the French countryside when she followed the authors' escape route in person. "Before I visited Chateau Feuga, where the Reys spent the fall of 1939, I had been picturing the black-and-white photo we found in the archives. But when I saw the house it was in full color! This, I think, is what surprised me—the black-and-white research versus the full-color scenes from my travels."

"I had been picturing the black-and-white photo we found in the archives. But when I saw the house it was in full color! This is what surprised me—the black-and-white research versus the full-color scenes from my travels."

Visiting another city to get an interview or to search for primary documents lifts you out of your sometimes-solitary writer's world to experience another lifestyle, language, climate, or geography. Russell Freedman prefers to have a first draft of the manuscript written before taking a trip. "Otherwise, you don't know what you're looking for." Images or impressions of a place will jump out at you because you have read about it first; you have prepared your mind to take in details you may not have noticed otherwise. No matter how temporary or vicarious the experience, you can still get a feel for how people live, even if they existed 200 years ago. When Jim Murphy was researching and writing *An American Plague* he visited Philadelphia and strolled down the narrow cobblestone alleyways. "On a hot summer day," he says, "you really can get a feel for how closed in and stifling that city must have felt back in 1793."

Fear Factor Research

Waiters in pleated white tuxedo shirts and crisp black bowties floated silver trays of appetizers through the crowd. Carefully, guests lifted a dolloped cracker or a stuffed mushroom from a platter as if they were removing wires from a bomb. We had in our hands what looked like sugar cookies with a candied cricket on top. As Peggy and I lifted them to our mouths, the cricket, encased in its amber shell of sugar, seemed to stare at us blankly. What was the best way to eat our entomological treats—bite it in half with our teeth, or pop the whole thing in at once? It was small and we both have big mouths, so we popped. We munched slowly, feeling spindly cricket legs snap against our molars. It was sweet, crunchy, and we have to admit . . . good!

"Fear factor" research is anything that takes you out of your comfort zone and gives you hands-on experience.

This entomological meal served at the Buffalo Museum of Science was one of our joint ventures into what Peggy calls "fear factor" research. It is anything that takes you out of your comfort zone and gives you hands-on experience. That night at the museum we nibbled on mealworm-stuffed mushrooms and garlic cricket canapés, and staked out the kitchen where bowls of writhing mealworms were being washed for the next course. It inspired both of us to write about eating insects—

something neither one of us would have even thought of if we hadn't done it ourselves.

My experience at the bug-eating party led me to write a picture book called *Bugs for Lunch*. It is a book in rhyme about animals and plants that eat insects, as well as how some people in poor countries, where meat is scarce, include insects in their diet. Peggy wrote an article called "Bugs for Breakfast." She did bookwork to learn about the eating habits of other cultures, and an interview with the museum's featured entomologist to learn about the study of entomophagy, but it took the actual eating of mealworms to give her article the punch it needed to be accepted by *Cricket* magazine.

You don't have to do anything as crazy as eat insects to jazz up your writing, but do look for opportunities to see and experience for yourself what you are writing about. If you are writing about flying an airplane, call the airport and make arrangements for someone to take you up. If you are writing about a wombat, a baboon, or a llama, visit a zoo, animal park, or farm where you might be able to handle or interact with one. That's how I met an unforgettable chimpanzee named Bobby.

It all started after I'd read an article about a woman doing research with chimpanzees at Ohio State University. I planned to write about it, but it would have been difficult to describe these wonderful animals and the graduate students who are studying them if we had not met them. Five-year-old Bobby made a big impression. When this young chimpanzee ran into the playroom he jumped on a mattress, just like a kid his age would. Then he untied my sneakers, and grabbed my notebook and pencil. I cherish my chimpanzee notes, which look like the scribbles of a pre-schooler. As we watched the older chimps answer questions on their computer screen, I knew I wouldn't have believed it if I hadn't seen it. I later wrote about Bobby in my book, *What Does the Crow Know?*

Another way to gain experience is to ask, "Can I help?" This tactic works especially well when dealing with agencies that are shorthanded.

Peggy tagged along to set up cameras in a bald eagle's nest, and helped excavate the bones of a mighty mastodon. I've quizzed math-minded parrots and worked on a biological research ship. The experiences we've had always proved invaluable to our research, and made us more invested in the writing process.

When Enough Is Enough

In an online interview, author Joanne Mattern once said, "I've heard fiction writers say that you should know more about your characters than you ever put on the page. In nonfiction, you should know more about your subject than you ever write about!" But how do you know when you have enough information for the book or article you want to write? Both Peggy and I research and write at the same time, so we never really stop researching until the final draft. But when you begin to come across the same facts and anecdotes repeatedly, it may be time to wrap up the research and focus on writing.

> When you begin to come across the same facts and anecdotes repeatedly, it may be time to wrap up the research and focus on writing.

No matter what amazing or fascinating material you turn up, remember that the *story* is most important. From your research you'll put together the skeletal framework of your story—the true characters, real setting, conflict, even dialogue—to create the nonfiction plot.

Facklam Files:
Margery's Trip of a Lifetime

Once in a blue moon, an unexpected event takes you to a whole new world. That happened to me when an editor asked me to write a book about the things that affect climate changes. I had little interest in the subject, but my husband, Howard, who taught biology, chemistry, and Earth science, loved anything to do with weather. Every day he checked his barometer, thermometer, the clouds, and the rain gauge, and listened to several weather reports. I tended to look out the window to see if I needed snow boots, an umbrella, or suntan lotion. But when Howard offered to help with the research, I accepted the job, never guessing where it would take us.

I was well into the book when I was stymied by a chapter on how ocean currents affect climate and weather. I read the chapter to my critique group, and one of the other writers said, "Marge, that's not very interesting. There's no story, no zip."

I wanted to say, "Well, I'd like to see you make ocean currents interesting," but I didn't. I wasn't sure how to fix it, but the next morning I looked through my notes and found the name of a professor at Duke University who was studying climate change. I hesitated to call him because I wasn't sure what to ask, but I called anyway. He was very kind, and explained that he was doing research on an ocean current called El Niño that runs along the Pacific coast of South America. Suddenly he said, "This would be easier to explain if you could see it firsthand. We're sailing for the Galapagos Islands with a group of scientists in a few months. Could you go with us?"

That was like asking Cinderella if she wanted to go to the ball. I'd been longing to see the Galapagos since I was in elementary school, but I told him we couldn't afford it. Then he said the magic words, "I meant, could you volunteer to help with the research? Have you ever done any graduate work?" I told him I had, but I still feel a tinge of guilt because I didn't tell him that the professor I worked for was studying porcupines.

Howard spent a week of his Easter vacation with me at the Darwin

Facklam Files:
Margery's Trip of a Lifetime (cont.)

Research Station on the island of Santa Maria in the Galapagos, then had to return to teaching. I then joined a team of scientists on the *Wecoma*, a small ship equipped to collect information on El Niño. I was seasick and half asleep for most of the first week because I was on the midnight to four A.M. watch, with another watch eight hours later in the day. Every four hours, the scientists lowered a huge computerized collecting device deep into the ocean. When it was hauled up, we took the vials of water, collected at different depths, to the ship's laboratory and analyzed them for chemical content and temperature, as well as animal and plant life.

Thanks to that amazing firsthand experience, my new chapter on ocean currents was fun to write, and certainly more interesting to read. Other experiences on that trip, such as visiting the Darwin Research Station, became a chapter in another book as well as a magazine article. That's one of the fascinating things about firsthand research: It's sometimes a bottomless bag of surprises.

Chapter 5
The Heart and Voice of Story

Plot ┄┄┄

┄┄┄┄┄ Setting

Voice ┄┄┄┄┄

Dialogue

"The best writers of nonfiction put their hearts and minds into their work. Their concern is not only with what they have to say but with how they say it."
—Milton Meltzer, author of *Voices from the Civil War*

While gathering reams of research, you might wonder what you'll do with all the information. How are you going to mold it into a form that will convey exactly what you want to say? At this stage, it is important to remember that you are writing a *story*, a word most people don't associate with nonfiction. So let's review what story really is and how you can use the elements of storytelling—plot, scene, dialogue, and voice—to get a reader's blood pumping.

Story is not just a fictional construct. In the broadest sense, a story is the recounting of events, whether real or imagined. Think about the last time you told friends about some horrific—or terrific—event that happened in your life. You told them how you felt and how it affected you. You described the people involved, hitting the high points and leaving out the boring bits. You wanted your friends to feel as if they had been there, so you automatically shaped the story to make it as compelling as possible. You told a nonfiction *story*. You presented facts in an interesting and organized way to connect with your audience. And that is what you must do when you write.

A story has a certain structure—a beginning, middle, and end. The major incidents are planned out or plotted to have the greatest impact, and the writer explores the motives behind the action. "Story makes a stab at explanation," says Beverly Lowry in an essay called, "Not the Killing but Why." It must be more than just reportage. It *must* make connections between cause and effect, and between the events and the reader's life. A nonfiction writer takes the raw facts and shows the reader what that data means. Author Phillip Hoose not only documents the demise of the Ivory-billed Woodpecker in *The Race to Save the Lord God Bird*, he explains the many factors that led to it: scientists who routinely shot birds to study them because they had no other method of close observation; wealthy bird collectors who were eager for rare stuffed specimens; the clear-cutting of habitat to feed a rapidly growing nation in need of lumber; and women's passion for stylish hats. Hoose tells us *why*.

> A nonfiction writer takes the raw facts and shows the reader what that data means.

Fiction writers make up every element of their imaginary stories, but the components of your true story are already there, you just have to recognize them. The characters are given to you. "If you are writing about bugs," says editor Randi Rivers, "then the bugs are the characters. How are you going to make them engaging?" Your setting is established. But how are you going to recreate a sense of place so that your readers can close their eyes and feel as if they are there? What unifying facts will you use to lead your reader through the details of the story? What pattern of information will you highlight?

Storytelling Techniques

Plan to use the same techniques that novelists use. Accurate quotes from interviews or other research will provide the element of dialogue, and careful descriptive detail will establish your setting of time and place. Combining these components and shaping your true story is what renowned nonfiction writer Gay Talese referred to as *choreography*. "When it comes to putting [the story] together it becomes a mosaic. It's prismatic; it moves around with different sections of light coming in." Your nonfiction manuscript may morph through several outlines and shape-shift through several drafts, but Talese assures us that, "When constructed in its final form, it seems simple and graceful. It's seamless; it doesn't show all of the previous calculated thinking that went into the juxtaposition of this and that."

Some writers create elaborate outlines while others write following some internal plan. There is no one way to do it. Caroline Arnold, the award-winning author of scores of nonfiction books for children, believes that an outline that tells you where you're starting, where you're going, and what stops are along the way is worth its weight in gold.

> Some writers create elaborate outlines while others write following some internal plan.

On the other hand, Peggy cringes when a publisher asks her to create an outline. She is certain that whatever she submits will be altered and adapted as she gets down to the business of fleshing it out. So she prefers Arnold's visual image that portrays the main theme as a clothesline. Each subtopic, like an item of clothing, is attached along its length. Since Peggy tends to write at home to the rhythm of the washing machine, this image sits well with her. It allows for the "unclipping" of one subtopic and sticking it further down the line if necessary.

But in some sense every writer does create an outline, a format, a form that is filled in gradually, whether it's on index cards, typed neatly with Roman numerals, or on freshly laundered pages floating invisibly between the synapses of your brain. So, the first order of business is to discover the structure of the information or the plot of your story.

Plotting Your True Story

Finding the right format may take some trial and error. Sometimes the story structure is clear—a person was born, grew up, did great things, and died. But how you shape a story may not always be apparent at first. You may have folders full of wonderful information but you can't use it all. What bits do you leave out? Where do you start and what comes second, third, and fourth?

As the writer you reveal information as you see fit. A journalist might tell a news story by revealing the order of events as they happened, but a nonfiction storyteller develops a plot. *Story* is the sequence of events as they happen. A *plot* is the sequence of events as the writer arranges them. This might involve foreshadowing events to come, or starting at the end.

Many biographies and historical accounts are told chronologically. Jim Murphy's recounting of the Chicago Fire of 1871 begins with Daniel "Peg Leg" Sullivan, the first person to notice a flame flickering in the O'Learys' barn. James Giblin, in his book, *Good Brother, Bad Brother*, begins his story of Edwin and John

> A *plot* is the sequence of events as the writer arranges them.

Wilkes Booth on April 14, 1865, in Boston. He places the reader in Edwin's dressing room just before he is about to go onstage to a sellout crowd. Perhaps Giblin did this knowing that we would be picturing the events going on at that same moment in another theater, the Ford Theater. He could have started this story in a number of places, but chose the moment when not only the brothers' lives, but also the lives of everyone in the nation changed. He then goes back to describe pertinent moments from the Booths' childhoods.

Many science books are structured cumulatively, layering information from simple to complex. In *What's the Buzz?* I started with the most basic question: What is a bee? With each chapter I added to the reader's knowledge as I laid out the research that scientists were conducting in Panama. With each question researchers answered, more questions cropped up. What do bees eat? How do bees find flowers? How do they communicate? How do they find food at night?

Bruce McMillan's book *Summer Ice* follows the food chain starting with algae and plants and moving up to krill, whales, penguins, and seals. This progressive pattern works well when introducing new ideas to a reader, for example describing a process such as the construction of a tennis racket, or step-by-step instructions to cook a meal.

You may find that two stories exist and you want to share both. In *They Came from the Bronx*, Neil Waldman writes parallel narratives that converge in the end—a Comanche boy and his grandmother remember the buffaloes of the past, while captive-born buffaloes from the Bronx Zoo journey to the open range of Oklahoma.

Your nonfiction piece might work better using another, nontraditional structure. Concept books, for example, employ an alternative plotline to get their message across. *Will a Clownfish Make You Giggle?* by Kay Dokken works well in its question-and-answer format because it plays off the quirky images that each unusual fish name evokes. Peter and Connie Roop's biography *Take Command, Captain Farragut!* is told in letters that the 12-year-old naval captain might have written home. Author and illustrator Kadir Nelson divides his book, *We Are the Ship: The Story of Negro League Baseball*, into nine innings, each covering a topic pertinent to the League; and Gene Barretta uses the teeter-totter concept of now and then for his book *Now & Ben: The Modern Inventions of Benjamin Franklin*. Of course, many authors have employed the alphabet because it provides the perfect picture book-sized layout for just about any subject.

Examine other children's books. What types of plotlines did the authors use? Are the stories chronological, cumulative, parallel, or based on a concept like a Q & A? Experiment with different structures until you have found the one that will best tell your story. It may take some time, but it will be well worth the effort. Once you have developed the plot, then you can use other storytelling elements to pull your readers into the narrative.

> You must give readers visual cues to guide their imaginations to a distant place or time.

Set the Scene

It is just as important to set the scene in nonfiction as it is in fiction because the setting is essentially another character. If the setting is vague, then the subject of a biography, for instance, seems to float in a timeless vacuum. You must give readers visual cues to guide their imaginations to a distant place or time.

Here is a passage from Phillip Hoose's *The Race to Save the Lord God Bird*. What picture builds in your mind as you read it?

> Alexander Wilson clucked his horse slowly along the margin of a swamp in North Carolina. Bending forward in the saddle, he squinted out at the small birds that flitted across the moss-bearded boughs of giant cypress trees, hoping he could get a clear shot without going into the water. When he heard the first call of an Ivory-billed Woodpecker, he knew what it was instantly, even though he had never seen one before. Here was the toot of a toy horn everyone had told him to expect, repeated again and again.

As clearly as a map, Hoose directs us to a location, North Carolina along the margin of a swamp. Can you hear the man cluck to his horse, and hear the distinct birdcall? We are even afraid to get our feet wet as we look up at the overhanging moss in the cypress trees. Hoose recreates a moment that happened in February 1809. And for that moment we are there. We would not have seen the same picture in our minds if Hoose had simply written something like this: "Alexander Wilson rode through the trees along a North Carolina swamp. He was about to fire his gun when he heard the call of an Ivory-billed Woodpecker." It is the same information, but not the same scene. Hoose effectively uses three techniques to recreate the setting:

- **Specific details.** The author does not rely on the reader's knowledge of North Carolina flora to tell us vaguely that the swamp had trees. He shows us cypress heavy with moss. Using specific details like the species of a tree allows your reader to build an accurate mental picture. In *Brooklyn Bridge*, Lynn Curlee explicitly describes the working conditions down in the caissons during bridge construction. "Light was provided by flickering blue-white gas jets and smoking whale oil lamps that cast eerie black shadows." And the men worked "stripped to the waist and wore rubber hip boots to get around." What specific information can you give your readers?

- **Concrete analogies.** Here's how Sy Montgomery describes the world of the tree kangaroo: "Cool clouds cloak the trees. Mosses and ferns, vines and orchids trail down from the branches—like the beards of old wizards." She creates a concrete image for her reader. We can see the moss hanging like an old wizard's beard. In *Brooklyn Bridge*, Curlee describes the cables of the bridge as "thicker than a very large man's waist." That is an "Oh, wow!" image.

- **All five senses.** Children learn better if they can see, hear, and touch the subject, so tingle those senses when you describe the setting. Hoose, for example, opens our ears. He lets us hear the rider cluck to his horse rather than tells us he prods his horse on. We hear a distinct toy horn toot and know we have heard the rare Ivory-billed Woodpecker.

You can employ the other senses, too. When you took notes at your last interview, did you jot down the odor that hit your nose as you entered the winning team's locker room, or record that feeling you got when you stepped into the cramped belly of a WWII submarine? Those sensory details will help you recreate the scene for your reader and establish a mood.

Setting the scene by using specific images and sensory details to transport your reader to another time or place is what it means to *show* rather than *tell*. "Show, don't tell" is a useful saying and a good one to remember. Don't *tell* us it is hot; *show* the sweat dripping off the man's brow. Don't *tell* us a frog is small; *show* it sitting on the thumbnail of a biologist. It is not clear who first came up with this advice, but it may have been Anton Chekhov, a Russian writer in the 1800s, who once wrote, "Don't tell me the moon is shining; show me the glint of light on broken glass."

Does that mean that you only show, and never tell? No. But it is a rule of thumb, one technique you can use to engage your readers and draw them in.

Quotes as Dialogue

Another storytelling element to use is dialogue. Not the imagined conversations that writers used to make up for biographies 50 years ago, but the voices of your real characters as revealed in actual quotes. While reading fiction we "hear" the characters through dialogue. We get to know their personalities, their motivations, and their interests. Plus we like the white space on the page that eases our eyes from long, dark blocks of description. The same is true in nonfiction. Let your readers hear the story through your characters' quotes.

"Don't tell me the moon is shining; show me the glint of light on broken glass."

Several authors have been very effective at creating books using quotations from primary sources. Their words provide the linking narrative that pulls readers along like a tram through a theme park, stopping at every exhibit to let a child listen to each individual account.

Jim Murphy, in his book *The Great Fire*, uses a number of distinct "voices" to create the patch-worked story of that fateful night in Chicago.

We hear from a cast of characters, including a 20-year-old newspaper reporter:

"Streams were thrown into the flame, and evaporated almost as soon as they struck it. A single fire engine in the blazing forests of Wisconsin would have been as effective as were these machines in [this] forest of shanties . . ."

We also hear from a 12-year-old girl trapped in an alley:

"My legs and arms and back [were] all burnt where my dress caught fire . . . The bricks were still hot—very hot—but I found that if I did not stop [moving] my feet were not burnt so bad."

Quotes from interviews can be just as effective as long as you select your quotes carefully. As in fiction, you don't want to bore your reader with trivial "chit-chat" that does not move the story along, or use quotes that repeat what has already been said. In "Soccer Spreads Hope," an article in *Faces* magazine, author Kathleen Wilson Shryock uses a quote from 13-year-old Nicolette Iribarne to voice the theme of the article. "The game of soccer led to instant friendship and showed me that beneath our cultural shields, our cores are all the same."

> Quotes, like illustrations or diagrams, should emphasize a specific point, support an argument, convey someone's personality, or provide unusual insight.

Quotes, like illustrations or diagrams, should emphasize a specific point, support an argument, convey someone's personality, or provide unusual insight. In *Freedom Riders*, Ann Bausum quotes liberally from civil rights activists John Lewis and Jim Zwerg. To support the point that the Freedom Riders' actions strained their relationships with their families, Bausum quotes Lewis: "I lost my family that spring of 1960. My mother made no distinction between being jailed for drunkenness and being jailed for demonstrating for civil rights." To convey the climate of the times Bausum quotes a congressman from Alabama who described the fate of the Freedom Riders like this: "Every decent Southerner deplores violence, but these trespassers . . . got just what they deserved." And Bausum lets Zwerg's own words provide a glimpse into a private and painful moment just before he was beaten unconscious: "I immediately felt a presence with me . . . And a calm and peace came over me that I knew if I lived or if I died, it was okay. It was gonna be all right."

Quote experts or primary sources when they present the information in an interesting way or paint a vivid picture. In his article, "Life on Ice" published in *Science World*, Michael Stroh quotes one scientist with a distinct voice kids can relate to when he says frozen frogs are ". . . no more alive than a pot roast." And in "On the Move," an article published in *National Geographic Kids*, Crispin Boyer relies on the words of expert Alan Rabinowitz to explain how a jaguar moves within its territory: "If you were charting a path to your friend's house or to someplace you haven't been before, you're not going to pick the most difficult way to go. Jaguars are the same way." Yet another example comes from a *Boys' Life* article by Jeff Piasky, "The Spin Doctor," which quotes a BMX rider as saying, "It's a scary feeling when you go up in the air, like you're on a roller coaster that's gotten loose."

If your source is not as articulate as you would like, paraphrase to get the flavor of their words instead of quoting directly. For example, the earlier quote could be paraphrased like this: *According to Rabinowitz, a jaguar uses the easiest path,* just as you would choose the most direct route to a friend's house. Preserve the general idea and your reader will still hear the personality and the voice of the speaker.

> If your source is not as articulate as you would like, paraphrase to get the flavor of their words instead of quoting directly.

Your Writing Voice

Here's a strange piece of advice: Write with your ear. Actually, learning to write with your ear is one of the most valuable techniques you can learn as a writer. It simply means that as you write, the voice you "hear" must be your own.

Early in my writing career, when I read the news that best-selling author George V. Higgins was going to teach a graduate seminar on writing at the University of Buffalo, I signed up. Even though I

> As you write, the voice you "hear" must be your own.

knew he didn't write for children, I didn't want to pass up the chance to learn from this outstanding author of gutsy crime stories. His most famous book, *The Friends of Eddie Coyle*, had been made into a prize-winning film. I was sure there would be standing room only, so I arrived early on the first day of class. It turned out there were only eight of us—four graduate students and four senior citizens.

Higgins settled in a chair beneath a No Smoking sign, and lit a cigarette. He took a deep drag and exhaled slowly. Then he said, "I'm going to read from the best book ever written."

He read the first chapter of *Charlotte's Web*.

When he wrote his book *On Writing*, Higgins gave this advice: "You can get what you need by shutting yourself in a room by yourself for 20 minutes a day and reading aloud from E. B. White's *Charlotte's Web*, and going on from there to other works of skill, until you begin to see, by hearing, how much the choice and arrangement of words contributes to the impact of the story, even when no sound is uttered in reading." And then he adds this about your own work, "Rely upon it: If you can read it aloud to yourself without wincing, you have probably gotten it right."

This "getting it right" is mostly about finding your voice. And voice is as vital to nonfiction as it is to fiction or poetry or song. It is also an elusive concept difficult to define. Polly Campbell wrote this description of voice in an article for *The Writer* magazine: "Voice is the piece of personality you leave on the page. It's the quality that gives your writing a memorable and distinctive sound. It's the unique way each writer writes. A well-developed voice elevates writing from the ranks of a factual report to a piece of compelling nonfiction." Technically, voice is the choice and placement of words, the rhythm and pace of the language, and a distinctive attention to detail and color. Some writers are naturally humorous and witty, others serious and thoughtful. Some are clear and direct while others have a more lyrical style. One is no better than another. It is simply a reflection of an individual's personality and point of view.

> "Voice is the piece of personality you leave on the page."

Be Yourself

The key to finding your voice is "Be yourself." That was my father's advice whether I was going to apply for a job or meet my future in-laws. And that's what you need to do when you write for toddlers, teens, or adults.

If you write technical reports or academic papers for a living, chances are these are written in the style and jargon of your profession. We found an example of professional jargon in a graduate school of education newsletter. The authors present workshops about "strategic writing instruction," which they describe in this paragraph:

> Strategic writing instruction consists of three types of knowledge (declarative, procedural, and conditional), which are incorporated into four instructional steps (identify a strategy, model it, scaffold the learning, and repeat the process). Such instruction helps struggling writers integrate default writing strategies (such as copying, narrating, and visualizing) with the text-based strategies (such as planning, paragraphing, and conforming to conventions). Imagine how video clips of teachers using strategic instruction help illuminate the meaning of that scheme.

In our view, this excerpt would have been more effective (and understandable) if the authors had written it in their own voice. We propose that literature created for any profession can and should be clear, concise, lively, and interesting to read.

We prefer the "strategy" described by writer Eric Blair, whose pen name was George Orwell of *Animal Farm* fame. In his essay, "Politics and the English Language," he came up with these rules to write by:

> (i) Never use a metaphor, simile, or figure of speech which you are used to seeing in print. (ii) Never use a long word where a short one will do. (iii) If it is possible to cut a word out, always cut it out. (iv) Never use a passive where you can use the active. (v) Never use a foreign phrase, a scientific word, or a jargon word if you can think of an everyday English equivalent. (vi) Break any of these rules sooner than say anything outright barbarous.

This advice is obviously written in the same no-nonsense voice that Blair used in writing his novel.

E. B. White, author of *Charlotte's Web*, wrote articles for the sophisticated *New Yorker* magazine in the same voice he used for his children's books. He may have chosen a different vocabulary, but he was always himself. C. S. Lewis was a historian and scholar at Oxford. He wrote brilliant books for adults. But he also wrote *The Lion, the Witch and the Wardrobe*, and other books for children in the Chronicles of Narnia series. All of his writing sparkles with his own elegant simplicity.

Author Laura Backes says, "Voice is the simplest thing in the world to learn, because it's already in you. But [it's also] the hardest to achieve, because it involves trusting yourself." And we all know how hard that is. When you begin to write, it is not unusual to be self-conscious about your work, or adopt someone else's voice. But essayist and novelist Anne Lamott says in her book *Plan B: Further Thoughts on Faith*, ". . . with writing, you start where you are, and you usually do it poorly. You just do it— you do it afraid. And something happens."

What happens is like jumping into a lake and finding the confidence to relax enough to float. The more you write, the more you will begin to relax and settle into your own voice.

Finding Your Voice

There are entire books devoted to developing a writer's voice, but most professional writers we spoke to felt that the key was the act of writing itself. The more you write the more distinct your voice will become. The flow of words, like the flow of water carving out a streambed, will define the voice within you.

> The more you write, the more you will begin to relax and settle into your own voice.

Don't second-guess yourself. Allow yourself to put your own perceptions on the page. As Tom Romano puts it in his book, *Crafting Authentic Voice*, you should "trust the gush." Get it all out on paper before you go back and revise. Assume that you are going to write what Anne Lamott dubbed the "shitty first draft." That is more than okay—it is to be expected. No one will see it but you.

We also recommend that you read. We agree with Walter Dean Myers, who believes that as you read you will set internal standards of what is good and what is great. Read what others have written so that you hear the subtle differences of each writer's voice. Read out loud.

And here is a bit of advice that we think gets overlooked by writers who are just starting out: Choose subjects that you care about. Your voice will become clearer in direct ratio to the amount of passion you have for the topic. Read the letters in the editorial section of your local newspaper and you can hear each writer's voice clearly. An ordinary citizen was compelled to speak out. Now think back to those high school writing assignments when the teacher told you what to write about. It was probably difficult to rally enthusiasm for the project, and most reports sounded the same. They lacked passion. They lacked voice.

Unique Voices

Here are a few passages from writers we admire. Listen to the rhythm of their sentences. Take note of the words they chose.

"In a time so long ago that only the rocks remember, the last glacier began to melt. As it turned to water, mountains of gravel trapped in the ice were dumped on the coast of New England. One mass, shaped like a flexed arm, is Cape Cod."
—Jean Craighead George, *The First Thanksgiving*

"Winds nudged and shoved the storm westward across the Atlantic. As it traveled, the storm fed on warm, moist air. It grew into a huge mass of dark clouds. Within the clouds, lightning crackled, thunder crashed and strong winds howled."
—Patricia Lauber, *Hurricanes*

"Sullivan ambled down the stretch of land between the O'Learys' and their neighbor, crossed the street, and sat down on the wooden sidewalk in front of Thomas White's house. After adjusting his wooden leg to make himself comfortable, he leaned back against White's fence to enjoy the night."
—Jim Murphy, *The Great Fire*

"Right from the start, Franklin was the center of his mother's world . . . And Sara was definite about what she wanted. She wanted her darling boy in dresses, so dresses it was. And she doted on his long golden curls, so curls it was. But Franklin was definite about what he wanted, too, and by six he wanted the curls off. Off they came!"
—Judith St. George, *Make Your Mark, Franklin Roosevelt*

"For a man who liked to ask questions, Leonardo da Vinci was born at the right time—April 15, 1452. Everybody was asking questions then. The age was called the Renaissance, a time of rebirth when people who had forgotten how to be curious became curious again."
—Jean Fritz, *Leonardo's Horse*

As you develop as a writer, it will become easier to write about all sorts of subjects, even ones you feel ambivalent about, because you will be confident that your well-established voice will be there.

A Voice Kids Hear

For children's nonfiction, a clear, casual voice is preferable to one that is condescending or exceedingly academic. Explaining technical information or difficult concepts to kids can be prime breeding grounds for condescension or for material that flies over the heads of your readers. Avoid the textbook voice with sentences that sound as if they were written by committee. Write as if you were talking to a child in your neighborhood.

One way to keep the writing grounded is to link complex concepts to a child's life. Draw parallels from the unknown to the known using metaphors and similes kids will recognize. In one issue of *Muse* magazine, Editor Diana Lutz explained the complex process of global warming by comparing it to a car heating up in the summer. "The windshield lets in the sun's radiation, which is absorbed and then reradiated . . . at wavelengths that do not pass as easily through the windshield as the incoming sunlight. So energy pours in but does not leave . . . In the case of the planet, the role of the window glass is played by trace gases in our atmosphere. . . ." Every kid who has burned his legs on the vinyl car seat will understand this concept.

> Avoid the textbook voice with sentences that sound as if they were written by committee.

Similarly, in *Kiki* magazine the job of a "fashion forecaster" was compared to a weather forecaster in Jane Carlin's article, "Fashion Forecasting": "You've grown up with weather forecasters and you know what they do—they predict if it will be rainy or sunny, hot or cold. A fashion forecaster's work is similar. The fashion forecaster predicts trends in fashion, such as the new colors, styles, and accessories." *Junior Baseball*'s Don Marsh revealed the secret to "boarding the mound" in "Hey Kid, Get an Attitude!" with this comparison: "Think of the pitcher's mound as the first piece of real estate you've ever owned. Take possession of it. Kick the dirt off the top. Grab the rosin bag, if there is one, and toss it out of the way . . . Make sure the mound is just the way you want it, before you throw the first pitch." Although owning real estate isn't something that kids have direct experience with, this parallel still succeeds in conveying the concept of taking ownership over something in a big way.

It Sounds Like an Encyclopedia

Here are two excerpts that describe the antlers of a deer. Listen to the difference in voice. Both provide detailed information, but one reads like a textbook and the other creates an image.

"Antlers are part of a deer's skull . . . The antlers' hard bony structure and sharp points make them extremely dangerous weapons. Male deer use them chiefly to fight for mates or for leadership . . . New antlers are soft and tender and grow rapidly. A thin layer of skin covers the antlers and contains blood vessels that stimulate growth."
—From *The World Book Encyclopedia*, Vol. 15

"In seeming madness, the young buck lowered his head in challenge. His little spikes shone like silver daggers. They had begun to bud in April and had grown all summer under a soft skin called velvet. By early September the spikes were hard and fully developed. Only a few days ago the spike buck had scratched the last tag of velvet from one spike and had polished them both on the trunk of a tree. Now he had turned from a gentle browser into a fighting warrior."
—From *The Moon of the Deer* by Jean Craighead George

You should also choose anecdotes with kid-appeal. In the Science of Saving Animals series for Millbrook Press, Peggy had to discuss DNA and how geneticists help conserve wild big cats. It required a lot of technical information that would be more palatable if wrapped in a kid-friendly story. Peggy found the perfect vehicle in a black Labrador named Moja.

She came upon Moja by accident, flipping through a wildlife magazine. A small current news clip caught her eye. It featured the work of Moja and his owner, Dr. Sam Wasser, a medical doctor and geneticist working at the Center for Wildlife Conservation in Seattle, Washington. Together they were collecting valuable data about the endangered lynx.

Moja's talent was sniffing out cat scat, or poop, in the forest. Trained like a police dog, Moja could track 13 different species at the same time, and locate scat from half a mile away and under as much as 12 feet of snow. This gift comes in handy when your prey is an endangered and elusive cat. By collecting and analyzing the DNA and other chemicals in the scat, Wasser could tell how healthy an animal was, if it was male or female, and if it was related to another animal—all the things

> "If I try to write with [too] little information, I find myself resorting to clichés and generalizations."

Peggy wanted to get across to her readers. Without a story like Moja's she would have had great difficulty explaining genetic research to middle-school students.

In order to find that perfect metaphor or anecdote you have to do thorough research. "If I try to write with [too] little information," Tom Romano says, "I find myself resorting to clichés and generalizations." You fall into the trap of padding your text with repetitious drivel that bores the reader. And that can lead to an excess of weedy words that need to be trimmed.

Kids like clarity. Vague words like *some, very, really,* and *sort of* prevent your clear voice from ringing out. Cut them out. Listen for unnecessary phrases that can be better said in a single word. Many writing students, for example, rely on the phrase "due to the fact that," to make their point sound more important. "Because" is clearer. It also lifts the information to a prominent place in the text.

Kids are active and they like active writing. Use strong words and phrases in place of wishy-washy ones. In Patricia Lauber's *Hurricanes* excerpt in the sidebar on p. 101, notice how the winds "nudged and shoved." She could have written "the storm moved west," but that would have been ho-hum at best. In *Faces* magazine, Jennifer Moore wrote that an African mother's "baby backpack" was at a height

> Kids are active and they like active writing. Use strong words and phrases in place of wishy-washy ones.

"just perfect for tickling her elbows." That phrasing conjures up the active image of baby and mother interacting, rather than simply a baby on a mother's back. Attract young readers' attention with writing that is as lively as they are.

Go to the library and pull out a selection of nonfiction children's books. Listen for the author's voice that leads you through the text. Can you envision the setting? What is the plotline? How does the author use the elements of fiction to reveal the true story? How would you have done it differently?

Molding your nonfiction into an engaging narrative using the techniques described in this chapter will take you far in the writing process, but there is still more to do. From the title to the lead to the very last line of prose, there are many components you'll need to assemble in order to tie your story together.

The Writer's Bookshelf:
On Storytelling and Voice

Crafting Authentic Voice by Tom Romano, Heinemann, 2004

Finding Your Voice: How to Put Personality in Your Writing by Les Edgerton, Writer's Digest Books, 2003

Follow the Story by James B. Stewart, Simon & Schuster, 1998

On Writing Well by William Zinsser, HarperCollins, 2006

The Sound on the Page: Style and Voice in Writing by Ben Yagoda, Harper, 2004

Writing for Story: Craft Secrets of Dramatic Nonfiction by Jon Franklin, Plume, 1994

Chapter 6

Assembling the Story Skeleton

Titles

┌--- Sidebars

└--- Leads

Endings

"The lead, like the title, should be a flashlight that shines down into the story."
—John McPhee, author of *Coming into the Country*

So far we have focused on story: finding the facts that form the basis of your narrative, choosing the most appropriate structure to convey that story, and using storytelling techniques to make it compelling for the reader. Now it's time to construct your nonfiction skeleton, paying particular attention to key elements of organization and style that draw the reader in, add interest, and enhance your book's credibility.

Elemental Parts

All books and articles, no matter how long or short, have the same basic elements—a fresh beginning, a memorable ending, and lots of fascinating facts in between. Many nonfiction books also offer additional information in the form of sidebars, an author's note, glossary, source notes, bibliography, and index. These details hold special appeal for librarians, teachers, and parents who select and purchase most children's books. Each nonfiction project will have specific needs, but a reader's first impression always starts with the title.

Titles

A title is more than just a nametag tacked at the top of the first page. In *Writing Naturally: A Down-to-Earth Guide to Nature Writing*, author David Petersen points out the work that a title is asked to do. "Like a barker, the title of your essay or book must attract attention and coax a disinterested audience in off the noisy media midway to view your show." That's a big job for just a few words, and it can be done in two ways.

You could flag down your readers with a no-nonsense title that gives a straightforward description of a book or article's content, like *All About Afghanistan*, or *Ten Tips to a Great Interview.* This kind of title leaves nothing to the imagination. Librarians, editors, and kids like the direct approach because there are no surprises. It is easy for a child writing a report on hurricanes to locate the right reference on the shelf, and, for a reader flipping through a magazine, a way to quickly identify its contents.

> "Like a barker, the title of your essay or book must attract attention and coax a disinterested audience in off the noisy media midway to view your show."

But the direct approach can sometimes be dull. We like the indirect approach, using a title that tickles the editor's curiosity when he sees it in a query letter, or catches the eye of a reader glancing at a magazine. Here are a few clever titles we found paging through several children's magazines: "Wanted: Knights" is the title of an article by Sean McCollum about serving as a knight in the Middle Ages; "Seventeen Going on 170" by Lars Anderson is about 17-year-old NASCAR driver Sergio Peña; and "Join the

Band" by William Stier is about selling wristbands for a cheerleading fundraiser.

Titles, whether direct or indirect, should be short and easy to remember, although Peggy and I have a title that could compete for the longest in the world: *The Kids' World Almanac of Amazing Facts About Numbers, Math and Money*. A 12-word title is silly and hard even for us to recall. Peggy and I were going to call it *The Numbers Almanac*, but the trademark had to be added and the editors felt that *math* and *money* should be thrown in as well.

A title should also reflect the tone of the piece. For example, the title *And Then There Was One* reflects the somber subject of extinction. "Slime Time" indicates that an article on snails is going to be lighthearted. Look through several magazines and see if you can judge the tone of each piece from just the title.

Good titles work for a number of reasons, but here are a few suggestions as to why some titles work better than others:

- Clever word play has resulted in some of our favorite titles. We love M. D. Usher's title for his biography of the philosopher Socrates, *Wise Guy*. Peggy's picture book about President Washington's life as a farmer is another example: *Farmer George Plants a Nation*.

- Alliteration makes a title fun to say and easy to remember. Say *The Big Bug Book* or *Creepy Crawly Caterpillars* ten times fast.

- Target the reader's sensibilities. Kids love everything gross, weird, or wild, so if it is appropriate to your topic, go for it. "Who Eats the Fish Head?" is an article that gives tips on table manners, and *Trucks: Whizz! Zoom! Rumble!* uses sound effects to grab a young child's attention.

- Identify a benefit to the reader. "A Tighter Tush in Ten Minutes" tells teen girls just what to expect from this article.

Unlike text, titles do not fall under copyright laws, although some series titles may be trademarked. That is the reason so many books have the same title. So don't worry if your title is already out there. You can still use it. However, books with the same title can be easily confused with each other, which may hinder promotion and sales. To avoid confusion, you may want to alter your title slightly, or use a subtitle.

Subtitles are a great way to combine a fun title with the no-nonsense kind and expand on the content of your book or article. Peggy's book, *Talking Bones: The Science of Forensic Anthropology*, used a subtitle to clarify the exact meaning of the title, and Usher used a subtitle for *Wise Guy: The Life and Philosophy of Socrates*. Subtitles can also be used to distinguish one common title from another. For her book, *Pocahontas*, Kathleen Krull used the subtitle *Princess of the New World* to differentiate her biography from others on the market.

> Subtitles are a great way to combine a fun title with the no-nonsense kind and expand on the content of your book or article.

Be aware that editors may also have an opinion in naming a book. *Spiders and Their Web Sites* almost got nixed because of a very literal-thinking editor who believed that every illustration would have to show a computer. When *Talking Bones* was revised, the editor changed the title to the businesslike *Forensic Anthropology* to bolster sales to a college audience. Because *Bird Watch* was a too-subtle play on words for a book on endangered birds, it was changed to *Bird Alert*.

No matter what kind of title you choose, the straightforward approach or a clever twist on the obvious, it should do one thing: make a child want to read the first sentence.

First Impressions

Although seldom written first, your lead paragraph is usually *read* first, and you want to create the best impression. We agree with William

Zinsser, who says to make your first sentence your best. Your lead should set the tone of the piece, and introduce your topic within the first paragraph or two. Following are several ways to snatch your readers from their reality and pull them into the world you have created on the page.

Be Direct

It may not be the most imaginative way to approach your lead, but readers who are looking for information appreciate a first paragraph that tells them what the article or book is about. There is no doubt about what you'll get when you read Kathy Kranking's *Ranger Rick* article, "Meet the Sponges." She spells it out in the first two sentences. "Hi! I'm Soggy Sponge. And I'm here to help you soak up some facts about my sponge-tacular family." The direct approach is especially effective in a self-help manuscript or how-to. On the first page of *How to Draw Things in Nature*, author Rob Court promises: "The easy steps in this book will help you draw things in nature for school projects or for fun." So be honest with your readers and tell them what they can expect.

> Plunk your readers down into a world they may not be familiar with.

Create a Scene

Plunk your readers down into a world they may not be familiar with. Let that scene introduce your subject matter. In *Marine Mammal Preservation*, Peggy placed readers at the edge of a canal in Florida so they could understand the plight of the manatee.

> A female manatee poked her nose out of the water for a breath of air, her nostrils looking like two of the holes in a bowling ball. She was huge, yet hidden in the murky water. Her calf nuzzled against her side as she fed on the lush sea grass growing along the edge of the canal.

They seemed so peaceful; unaware of the dangerous world they lived in. Just a few yards away, a family fished from the canal wall with baited hooks, litter blew in the wind, and boats cruised noisily out to open water. This was the home of one of the most endangered marine mammals in the United States.

The same technique works in Ted Keith's *Sports Illustrated for Kids* article, "Taming the Tiger." To introduce young readers to the world of a sports star the piece begins:

Rookie ace Justin Verlander of the Detroit Tigers snakes his way through the visitor's clubhouse at Boston's Fenway Park. When he reaches his locker, there is a box waiting for him. He rips it open to find a brand-new baseball glove. He turns around and is handed another box, this one containing brand new shoes. . . . "So how's life in the big leagues, Justin?" "Pretty good," he says with a smile.

Share your own experiences with your reader. I remember waking up years ago to this scene so I used it as the lead to my article about daddy longlegs:

One summer morning, we found thousands of daddy longlegs dancing up the sides of our cottage at the beach.
"Spiders!" my brother yelled. "Where did they all come from?"
But daddy longlegs are not spiders, and even scientists aren't sure why they gather in such big bunches now and then.

Address Your Reader

In *Berry Smudges and Leaf Prints*, Ellen B. Senisi tells kids, "Think of your favorite place outside. Now imagine that place without color—any color at all." In this how-to book, the kids are part of the narrative right away. And in *American Cheerleader*, Jessica Spitale hooks her female readers in "No More Excuses!" with this reality check: "So you want to cheer, but . . . Well, you'll never earn a coveted spot on the team with that attitude! If you're more prone to making excuses than making it to tryout, *AC* knows exactly what you need: a pep talk." Instantly the reader's emotions have been tapped.

Facklam Files:
Peggy Finds a Lead at Last

Your lead might not come to you right away. Sometimes you must skip the beginning and come back to the opening once you have mastered your subject in later pages. When I was writing *Talking Bones*, the editors wanted the first chapter to be historical and discuss the early years of the science. I could not begin the book as I had originally planned, with the most compelling current murder to hit the news.

The first case that involved an anthropologist taking the stand was a grisly tale of a sausage maker who murdered his wife. It would certainly capture the attention of my readers, but how to begin? Quotes from the anthropologist were academic and uninteresting, and would have been difficult for middle-grade students to comprehend. Recreating the scene was a possibility, as it took place in a sausage factory, but the historic details were sketchy at best.

I was almost finished with the book and I still didn't have my first paragraph. Then I sent away for more background information from the *Chicago Tribune*'s archives and received in the mail a stack of photocopies from articles written in 1897. It was there that I found my lead, not on the front page or in any hard news column, but tucked away in the society section alongside wedding announcements. A small unobtrusive article cited the popularity of a new jump rope rhyme that kids were singing in the streets.

> "Old man Luetgert made sausage from his wife.
> He turned up the steam. She began to scream.
> There'll be a hot time in the old town tonight."

With a gruesome jump rope rhyme as my opening line, I could introduce the murder of Louisa Luetgert, illustrate just how consumed the citizens of Chicago were with this case, and proceed with the investigation that followed. My readers would instantly know that this was not going to be a boring recitation of forensic facts, but a collection of compelling stories that would make the material exciting and memorable.

Lead with an "Oh, Wow!" Fact

Make your reader think, "Oh, wow!" by leading with an amazing fact, statistic, or event. April Pulley Sayre begins *Coral Reef* with this thought-provoking sentence: "The water that makes up more than two-thirds of your body weight, that flows in your blood, that bathes your cells, and that you cry as tears, may once have flowed in a river . . . or been drunk by a dinosaur from an ancient lake."

And in *Bacteria and Viruses* Peggy starts with this unsettling statement: "We are not alone. No matter how clean we are or how healthy we feel, we carry around on our bodies billions of microbes . . . There are more than six hundred thousand bacteria living on just one square inch of skin, and an average person has about a quarter of a pound of bacteria in and on his body at any given time." An "Oh, wow!" fact grabs your readers' attention and makes them want to read more.

> A well-phrased question pulls readers right into the text by making them part of the story.

Ask a Question

A well-phrased question pulls readers right into the text by making them part of the story. *Sea Horse: The Shyest Fish in the Sea*, by Chris Butterworth, begins, "In the warm ocean, among the waving sea-grass meadows, an eye like a small black bead is watching the fish dart by. Who does it belong to?" What kid wouldn't keep reading to find the answer?

In a horse magazine, this leading question is sure to elicit a positive response: "Was there ever a horse that touched your heart so deeply you knew instantly he would be a lifelong friend?" Now the reader is primed to hear another horse-fancier's love story.

In the *Boys' Quest* article, "Perfect Pet Pictures," author Lisa Hart starts by asking readers, "Could your mutt be too magnificent for megabytes? Are you having trouble capturing your cat's inner animal on film?" This lead grabs attention in a humorous way and sets the tone for the article's lighthearted look at pet picture-taking.

When asking a question at the beginning of your text, make sure it is a question that will prompt curiosity or a definite yes. You don't want to ask a question and have the reader say "No," and close the magazine.

Make 'Em Laugh

Kids love humor, so I used a joke as a chapter opener in my book, *Who Harnessed the Horse?* "What was the world's first vending machine? The cow, because you put grass in one end and milk comes out the udder." But you don't need an actual joke to put a smile on your reader's face. Sarah Kwak used a lighthearted approached in her article, "Miracle on Ice: The Next Generation," about father and son hockey players. "Ryan Suter never had to worry about what to bring to school for show and tell. When you have an Olympic gold medal lying on the kitchen counter at home, the choice is easy . . ."

Dan Risch's profile of origami artist Robert Lang in *Odyssey* begins with a "WARNING! Reading further may lead to uncontrollable folding of class reports into cootie catchers and hopping toads. Look for these symptoms: folding of scraps of paper into stars, the urge to figure out puzzles, and improved math skills. If left unchecked, a passion for origami may lead to designing vehicle airbags and space telescopes. Should symptoms persist, see your math teacher for directions on how to fold an origami bunny—and for band-aids, as needed." Few teenagers wouldn't want to keep reading after that introduction. If your subject lends itself to a little jest, a humorous lead might be the right approach.

> If your subject lends itself to a little jest, a humorous lead might be the right approach.

Start with a Quote

If you can't say it any better, let your subject speak for itself. Susan Campbell Bartoletti uses primary sources extensively, and she began

Growing Up in Coal Country with the words from one unknown coal miner to illustrate the absurdity of sending young boys to work in the mines.

> At the age of eight, I left school and was given a job in the mines. I found it pretty hard getting out of bed at five-thirty every morning. The first two months, the road to work wasn't bad, but with the coming of snow, I found that I was much too small to make my way to work alone. Many times I was forced to wait by the side of the road for an older man to help me through the snow. Once I was lifted to the shoulders of some fellow miner and carried right to the colliery.

Sometimes a short quote is even more effective. A striking one-liner can set the tone for what's to follow, and lead readers smoothly into your story. When writing her article, "Chemical Foams in the Line of Fire" for *ChemMatters* magazine, Myrna Zelaya-Quesada knew that her ultimate goal was to explain the underlying chemistry and technical details of firefighting foams, but she also tried to bring the story to life for young readers. She wanted to offer more than the images of forest fires that were provided during a television news report. One such quote from a retired fire chief gave her just what she was looking for:

> "I could see the big fireball rolling across the sky from treetop to treetop, and the winds it created just roared like a tornado." Retired Deputy Chief Jim Tuma was describing his unforgettable first-hand experience fighting the wildfire that burned 450 acres of the dense ponderosa pine forest near Los Alamos, NM, in May 2000.

This quote has two things going for it: it is authoritative (from a fire chief who's been there) and attention-getting. If you are lucky enough to get a relevant quote that inspires, enlightens, or explains an aspect of your topic in an interesting way, consider making it your lead.

If you do not have an appropriate quote, don't invent dialogue. That technique was used in nonfiction books many years ago, but is now frowned upon by editors, librarians, and teachers who prefer accuracy to fictitious dramatized accounts.

First Sentences

Here are five examples of first sentences from biographies about Ben Franklin. Notice how different authors introduce this amazing man. How would you begin?

"Now and then, we think about Ben. Dr. Benjamin Franklin, to be precise. And we think about his many inventions—inventions he originated more than two hundred years ago."
— *Now & Ben: The Modern Inventions of Benjamin Franklin*, Gene Barretta, 2008. (The use of *we* includes the reader in the story.)

"The skies that June day in 1752 were dark and stormy in Philadelphia. Most people stayed inside their homes to keep dry. But not Benjamin Franklin. There he stood in the wind, the rain, and the lightning. And he was flying a kite!"
— *Time For Kids*, "Benjamin Franklin: A Man of Many Talents," Editors of *TIME For Kids*, 2005. (Recreates the scene.)

"Who was Ben Franklin?"
— *Who Was Ben Franklin?* Dennis Brindell Fradin, 2002. (Asking a question arouses curiosity.)

"Courteous Reader: Ben Franklin once said, 'A man's story is not told solely by a list of his grand accomplishments, but rather by his smaller, daily goods.'"
— *Ben Franklin's Almanac: Being a True Account of the Good Gentleman's Life*, Candace Fleming, 2003. (A quote from the subject himself adds interest.)

"Ben Franklin never watched TV . . ."
— *Benjamin Franklin: Scientist and Inventor*, Eve Feldman, 1990. (For a child this is an "Oh, wow!" fact.)

Happy Endings

Unlike fictional stories, you can't bring the crew of the *Challenger* safely back to Earth, or give the Native Americans back their land. You have to be true to the facts. But you still want to end on a positive note. Crafting an end to your nonfiction piece is just as important as writing the beginning.

We were all taught in high school English class to restate in the conclusion what we described in the body of the essay, but that is no longer a rule we need to abide by. If your young readers were diligent enough to read your entire nonfiction book or article (a fact we sometimes doubt given the attention span of children today), they already have taken in what you wanted them to know. So now you just need to lead them back to their world, the one that lies on the other side of the closed cover.

> Unlike fictional stories, you can't bring the crew of the *Challenger* safely back to Earth, or give the Native Americans back their land. But you still want to end on a positive note.

One way to do that is to come full circle. Remember the daddy longlegs lead? This is how that article ended: "Those dainty daddy-longlegs that swarmed over our cottage one summer were doing us a favor. They were eating thousands of tiny flies and other insects. We never saw so many of them in one place again, but whenever we do meet a daddy-longlegs, we always treat it kindly."

After two pages of sound advice on cheerleading tryouts, Spitale's "No More Excuses!" article throws it back to the reader. "Don't let the opinions of others or the fear of the outcome hold you back from following your heart. You don't want to look back and think, 'What if?'"

Peggy likes to use a strong quote at the end of a story because it is similar to a fiction writer letting the main character have the last word. For her title, *Post-Traumatic Stress Disorder*, she let scientist Ronald Duman at the National Center for PTSD sum up the future of his research: "There's enormous potential for the future to be able to go into the brain and fix things. That is certainly the goal—just figuring out how to do it is the question."

Catherine Thimmesh effectively ends *Team Moon* with a quote from astronaut Neil Armstrong thanking all the Americans who worked on the project, which finishes with ". . . Good night from *Apollo 11*."

Although you don't want to restate your objective, you do want the reader to know that the promise of the piece has been met. For example, the subtitle of Crispin Boyer's article about jaguars, "On the Move," says, "How Conservationists Are Helping Jaguars Make a Dangerous Journey." Boyer keeps that promise by finishing with one jaguar's safe arrival. "The big cat is satisfied with what he sees, smells, and hears in his new territory. His journey has come to an end. He is home."

Each chapter ending is also important. Like a novel, you want to lead your readers into the next chapter to keep them reading. You aren't doing your job unless your audience gets yelled at for reading past their bedtime. One way to make them turn the page is to ask a question. In *Plants: Extinction or Survival?* I draw readers into the next chapter by describing the plight of famine-stricken nations whose crops were depleted, and then asking, "So what's being done about it?" They have to keep reading to find out.

> You aren't doing your job unless your audience gets yelled at for reading past their bedtime.

Sidebars

An easy way to highlight information is to place it in a sidebar. On the printed page this information is offset in a box, similar to a picture with a caption. Peggy's Science of Saving Animals series uses sidebars to highlight natural history information about specific animals that are discussed in the main body of the text. Rather than interrupting the story of tracking the North Atlantic right whale to convey this information, the whale's size, population numbers, feeding habits, and other facts are placed in a sidebar so that kids who are looking for that information can find it quickly.

Material in a sidebar can be written in a few short paragraphs or as a list, bulleted or numbered for easy reading. Look at the sidebars in this book to see the wide variety. Think of a sidebar as an accessory for your well-dressed article. Typically it is short, less than 500 words.

Short sidebars work especially well in how-to books and articles. *Pack-O-Fun* magazine uses small sidebars, sometimes called tip boxes or text boxes, to present one- or two-sentence short cuts and tips related to a set of craft instructions. Other creative sidebar uses in this magazine include "Did You Know?" sidebars with relevant factual tidbits related to the craft, and "More Fun Stuff" sidebars with websites about the products used within the craft.

Magazine editors in particular appreciate the addition of sidebars because they provide a visual as well as textual element to the piece. Some publications even pay separately for sidebars. As a result, the word count for sidebars is usually not part of the total word count, but record-ed separately.

Some publishers have a format for indicating sidebars in your manu-script. If a format is not specified, then place your sidebars at the end of your manuscript on a separate page labeled SIDEBARS. If you have more than one, each should be labeled separately and titled. Titles can be cute and catchy or simple and direct. Look through the magazine you're targeting to see what kind of sidebars it features. For a book, you might have many side-bars. Note where they should be placed within the text using bracketed headings that say [SIDEBAR BEGINS] and [SIDEBAR ENDS], to differenti-ate them from the rest of the text.

> Magazine editors in particular appreciate the addition of sidebars because they provide a visual as well as textual element to the piece.

Served On the Side: What to Put in a Sidebar

1. Fast facts about your topic.

2. Instructions for an accompanying craft or science project.

3. An additional human-interest story that relates to your subject. If you are writing about the general topic of ecology you could highlight a person or community that recycles in a new or surprising way.

4. A list of websites, addresses, or phone numbers of organizations or agencies readers can contact for more information.

5. A checklist readers can refer back to, such as "10 Items to Take to College."

6. Selected quotes that will capture your readers' attention.

7. Definitions of words that are used in the text. By putting definitions in a sidebar you'll avoid bogging down your article.

8. A short quiz.

At the Back of the Book

To accessorize a book further, you may want to include additional information at the end of your manuscript. This material is called back matter and may include an author's note, glossary, time line, source notes, further reading list, bibliography, and index.

The back matter in a book, or the lack of it, is one way a librarian or reviewer judges a nonfiction book's quality. Library director Marie Bindeman admits that a nonfiction children's book "without source notes or a glossary is something that really riles a librarian," because these features are the tools they use to scrutinize books worthy of purchasing with their ever-dwindling budgets. She also reminded us that they are "the tools that help make the book more accessible to the reader." A time line, for example, puts the events that you discussed in detail into a quick reference chronology. A list of further reading gives readers a handy jumping-off point for their own exploration. So think about what supplementary information would be useful to your readers.

Author's Note

Do you have a compelling story about how you did your research? It might make an interesting author's note. Or perhaps you need to clarify difficult concepts or events that could not be fully explained in the main body of the text without taking away from the story line. For example, in her author's note for *When Marian Sang*, Pam M. Ryan notes that Marian Anderson had been criticized for not being a stronger activist and tells how she struggled to find a balance between her career and equality.

> A list of further reading gives readers a handy jumping-off point for their own exploration.

In *Farmer George Plants a Nation*, Peggy added an author's note about Washington's views on slavery because it is too important a topic to be lost or glossed over in the narrative flow of the main body of text. By placing it in a separate section, Peggy was able to give it the attention it deserved.

If a biography, for example, only covers a portion of a person's life, the author's note gives you the chance to fill in the blanks. Who did he marry, how many children did she have, etc. Peggy's biography of naturalist Roger Tory Peterson called *For the Birds* highlights the early years, so she added a note listing honors and awards he received later in life. Another note suggests what the reader can do to carry on Peterson's legacy.

Lincoln was a man of many words, so leaving the reader with a sampler of quotations seems the logical thing to do in *Lincoln: A Photobiography.* Of the quotes that Russell Freedman includes in the back matter, this one could easily apply to writers: "Always bear in mind that your own resolution to succeed is more important than any other thing."

Glossary

Does your book introduce new vocabulary? A glossary gives the definition of these words. Most editors recommend that the words in the glossary should be used more than once throughout the book so they become part of the child's vocabulary, however, Bindeman acknowledges that, from a librarian's point of view, a glossary might not be needed if you adequately define key words within the text.

> Time lines are especially useful to encapsulate the events in a person's life or the development of a product, or to showcase the cause and effect of related events.

Some educational publishers may provide you with age-appropriate lists of vocabulary words that are used in a particular series, but we have not found a need for vocabulary lists when writing magazine articles or stand-alone books.

Time Line

A time line is a useful visual reminder of key dates. In *Brooklyn Bridge*, Lynn Curlee includes a time line to effectively show how long it took to construct what was considered at that time to be "the eighth wonder of the world." Time lines are especially useful to encapsulate the events in a person's life or the development of a product, or to showcase the cause and effect of related events. Timelines can be written out in a vertical list or as a horizontal line across the page. In the Blue Banner Biography, *Stephenie Meyer*, Tamra Orr briefly lists 12 key years in Meyer's life, including the publication of *Twilight*. However, the time line at the back of Frances E. Davey's book, *A Brief Political and Geographic History of Europe*, is quite extensive, covering four pages and spanning more than 2,000 years. To help the reader better visualize the march of historical events, Davey includes a horizontal time line in every chapter. Running along the bottom of each page, this time line is punctuated with important dates that Davey discusses at length in the text above.

Be creative. Author/illustrator Marjorie Priceman wrote her time line in full paragraphs and used it to decorate the end pages of *Hot Air: The (Mostly) True Story of the First Hot-Air Balloon Ride.* A time line doesn't even have to be straight. Depending on the subject, it can swoop and swirl across the page as it does in *Mermaid Queen* by Shana Corey, showing swimwear fashions over the decades.

Bibliography

Every book and magazine editor will want to see a thorough list of your sources upon submission. Source lists are usually done in the typical bibliographic format, in alphabetical order, and can be divided under subheadings of books, periodicals, online sources, and interviews.

> Be creative. A time line doesn't have to be straight. Depending on the subject, it can swoop and swirl across the page.

There are several ways to cite your resources in the back matter. Your editor may require a complete bibliography, a selective bibliography, end notes, or a combination of these. It may be called "Works Consulted," "Sources," or "Bibliography." Check to see what your publisher prefers.

Generally, nonfiction picture books for the very young reader do not include a bibliography at all. But for school-aged children, including a brief bibliography of your most important sources will reflect the thoroughness and accuracy of your information.

Books for middle-grade readers and young adults need a more extensive bibliography, broken down into books, periodicals, online information, and interviews. If your editor does not specify the format, use the widely accepted *Chicago Manual of Style* notation.

Books with many quotations may need a citation or end note for each quote. This can be done using a superscripted number just after the quote in the text, which corresponds to the bibliographic information at the end of the book. Here is an example:

"When the first reference to a source is given, complete information about it should be included in the footnote . . ." [1]

At the end of the book you would find this citation:

1. Quoted in Vincent F. Hopper et al., *Essentials of English*, 5th edition, New York: Barron's, 2000. p.199.

An alternative to the superscripted endnote, which may seem too formal, is to cite all quoted material in a single list, noting page number and the first portion of the quote:

Chapter 6
p. . . . "When the first reference . . ." Vincent F. Hopper et al., *Essentials of English*, 5th edition, New York: Barron's, 2000. p. 199.

Further Reading Lists

For a child who is writing a report or who is hooked on the subject, the most useful section in the back of your book might be the "Further Reading" list. Sometimes titled "For More Information," this brief list includes other children's books similar in reading level to yours that are related to the subject.

Choose books that are current so that a child is likely to find them in the school or public library, and select those that speak directly to your topic as well as titles that explore related themes. You may just give a bibliographic list or an annotated list with a comment or two about why you recommend that particular title.

Reliable and kid-friendly websites are also welcome additions to this list. Your book will stand on the shelf for several years so make sure the websites you suggest are long-standing and reputable. Government agencies, museums, and educational institutions are good candidates.

Index

Middle-grade and longer texts will need an index. Proper names of people, places, and major events are usually cited in the index, as are the major ideas and concepts of the book. Some publishers will offer you the job of developing an index for additional compensation; others will pay someone else to do it. Depending on the length of the book, it is sometimes worthwhile to let someone else handle the index. It is a tedious and time consuming job. However, a freelance editor might not cite the information the way you would. If you are doing the index yourself using the page proofs or galleys, note each subject and what page it falls on. Your editor should provide you with the publisher's indexing guidelines, or you can consult a reference book such as *Indexing Books* by Nancy C. Mulvany.

> Proper names of people, places, and major events are usually cited in the index, as are the major ideas and concepts of the book.

The Structure of a Series

Many educational publishers require all of their series writers to work within the same format and write with a similar style. Peggy wrote two books for Lucent's Library of Science and Technology, but before she got a contract, the editors sent her more than a dozen pages of style guidelines. Each chapter had to be almost identical in word count and the theme development and narrative had to be declared ahead of time. They insisted on unified paragraphs, and no slang or clichés. Among the other rules: no foreshadowing, no contractions, and no sentences starting with *and*, *so*, or *but*.

Her experience with Pearson Learning Group was similar. This curriculum publisher's guidelines specified the number of words per line, lines per page, "phonics patterns" (for example specifying the inclusion of words ending in *–ing*), high-frequency word lists, embedded text structure (for example, the inclusion of cause and effect phrases like *because* or *if—than*), and writing to exacting reading levels.

From the publisher's point of view these strictures are necessary when a different writer produces each book in a series. Tight guidelines ensure that all the books will have a similar feel, and also assure librarians that each book will follow a similar pattern and provide a certain amount of information in a particular way. Teachers are able to differentiate which books are appropriate for the abilities of their students. There are no surprises.

> "It's like a puzzle where everything must fit."

These educational assignments are the bread and butter for many writers. But it can be intimidating the first time you receive the writer's guidelines with all the educational jargon. When writer Mary Scarbrough received her assignment she noted that, "The pages of guidelines far outweighed the eventual length of the book." But she liked the challenge of making all the parts of a leveled reader come together. "It's like a puzzle where everything must fit."

You might think it is difficult enough to write a strong manuscript without having to jump through these extra hoops as well. Just take a deep breath and relax. All the material you need to succeed is provided for you. Your editor will give you a sample outline and manuscript to look at; send you age-appropriate word lists for reference; and tell you how many sidebars to include and whether or not to use headings. Don't let the publisher's stated goals alter your writing style. The guidelines may mandate content that supports the National Council of Teachers of Mathematics Algebra Standard or teaches the comprehension of cause and effect, but your goal is to write a clear and exciting text. Those larger goals will naturally fall into place as you write, because the guidelines have already assured it.

You don't need to be an expert in "lexicon leveling" or adhering to a specific reading level. The editor will provide you with access to a website where the reading level of your manuscript is analyzed instantly. The manuscript can be easily formatted on your computer so that your margins keep you within the proper number of words per line or characters per line. Make yourself a checklist of all the requirements and keep your writer's guidelines on your desk for quick reference. Once you begin to write, you'll find that your natural writing style works well within their guidelines with only minor adjustments.

Writing for Readability

Publishers dictate the reading level of series to enable teachers and librarians to accurately select books their students can read and understand. The resulting text won't be too difficult or too easy. The reading level is measured primarily by sentence length and word frequency. For example, this short sentence needs a reading age of nine years. This longer sentence, which contains polysyllabic words and an adjectival clause, requires a reading age of more than 16 years.

As we mentioned before, if your editor needs to know your text's readability, he or she will most likely give you access to an online calculator. But if you are curious about the reading level of your writing there are a range of options available, including calculations you can do by hand, pricey software you can purchase, free online calculators, and an easy-to-use readability tool in Microsoft Word's Grammar Check feature. All of these tools are based on one of several standards like the Flesch-Kincaid standard, or SMOG, affably dubbed the Simple Measure of Gobbledygoop.

They all analyze your text for the number of words per sentence, syllables per word, syllables per sentence, etc., to arrive at a score. For example, Grammar Check scored this paragraph at a twelfth-grade reading level on the Flesch-Kincaid scale. There are five sentences per paragraph, 26.6 words per sentence and 4.8 characters per word.

Adjusting the reading level down is as easy as shortening sentences and replacing large words with ones that have fewer syllables. For example, you could replace the word *inquired* with the word *asked*. To raise the reading level, replace small words with larger ones and incorporate more compound sentences. Just because you are writing about dinosaurs for first-graders doesn't mean you need to avoid names like Diplodocus or Ichthyosaurus. But you might define *carnivore* in the sentence by adding the term "meat-eater."

Contextual cues from pictures or surrounding sentences help a young reader decipher the meaning of a new word. For example, the illustration accompanying the text about carnivores might show a T. Rex chewing on a Triceratops, and the passage might read: "The Tyrannosaurus was a carnivore. It ate plant-eating and other meat-eating dinosaurs."

Do not spend too much time worrying about the readability or reading level of your manuscripts. Read enough children's books and magazines and you will get a good sense of the clarity and vocabulary that is necessary to get your point across.

For one publisher, Peggy had to adjust her writing style to avoid speaking to the reader directly. This style was awkward, especially when she was writing about something as intimate as millions of bacteria living on a person's skin. In her own voice Peggy would have told the reader, "Microbes hide under your fingernails, lurk between your teeth, and live in your hair. At any given time you have more than six hundred thousand bacteria living on one square inch of skin." But series guidelines dictated that she speak to the reader in the third person. "Although they cannot be seen, microbes hide under fingernails, lurk between teeth, and live in hair. There are more than six hundred thousand bacteria living on just one square inch of skin, and an average person has about a quarter of a pound of bacteria in and on his or her body at any given time." It is a subtle difference, but this style tends to put science at arm's length, rather than reveal the world that lies right on the reader's doorstep—or skin.

> Nothing feels better than being asked, "Are you available to work on another assignment?"

At the end of the book Peggy wanted to let readers know that they had the opportunity to react to the world around them. She mentioned this fact to her editor on the project, who allowed Peggy to end the book using "we": "Bacteria and viruses are our worst enemies, yet they are also vital for our survival. We live in a sea of invisible microbes and we can either sink or swim."

The advantage of writing for educational publishers is that once you have successfully written one book for a particular publisher it is much easier to write additional titles for that publisher's list. And nothing feels better than being asked, "Are you available to work on another assignment?"

Chapter 7

Breathing
Life into Biographies

Picture Book Biographies ----┐

Choosing a Subject ----┐

└--- Contemporary Profiles

└--- Collective Biographies

"Choosing a subject for a biography may be as perilous or as charmed as a marriage. A writer chooses with fingers crossed."
—Sid Fleischman, author of *Sir Charlie*

There's nothing more intriguing than the life of another person. If that were not true, it's likely there'd be no *Oprah* or other talk shows, gossip columns, and of course fascinating biographies. A biography is the re-creation of a life, a balancing act of facts within a framework of story; it is finding that framework that is the hidden talent of a successful biographer.

Biography is the nonfiction genre that seems closest to fiction because it is structured around character, and lends itself easily to narrative storytelling. But an overly zealous biographer may get so carried away with every detail of the person's life that the manuscript becomes a monotonous list of events that happened at the age of two, three, and so on. To bring meaning to your presentation, follow esteemed biographer Milton Meltzer's advice: "The mind of the biographer must be free to seek some arrangement or pattern in the life he or she has studied. The biographer makes connections, holds back some facts, and foreshadows others . . . to impose a design upon chronology."

The design that emerges is made up of all those critical moments in your subject's life that shed light on the inner character and the motivation that led him or her to become a human rights activist, a famous author, a brilliant artist, the first to climb Mount Everest, or a lauded president. That is the narrative thread that runs throughout the person's life and your biography.

In their book, *Thinking Like Your Editor*, authors Susan Rabiner and Alfred Fortunato call this narrative the "mind story." "What brings the subject most vividly to life for the reader is this pattern . . . the consistent or inconsistent way he dealt with life's challenges, from tension to resolution, in each moment of crisis." By focusing on this pattern or outstanding characteristic you escape the impulse to include every inconsequential detail, and your biography will be much more accessible to young readers.

> Any person who is studied in school is a good subject for a biography.

Ordinary People

According to Gina Shaw, Editorial Director at Scholastic Inc., any person who is studied in school is a good subject for a biography, and other editors concur. In its writer's guidelines, Enslow Publishers asks writers to "submit biographies of influential people, both historical and contemporary. We want to see the lives and work of scientists and inventors." If there is a secret formula for writing a biography, that's it: "We want to *see* the lives."

Cast your net wide. Check on Amazon to see who has already been immortalized in a children's biography. An Internet search may turn up one book or one hundred, but even if there are several new books about the person you've chosen, don't be discouraged. There may be a place for another, especially if your book will cover different aspects of the subject's life, be aimed at a different age group, contain new information, or take an unusual slant. The Wright Brothers are a popular topic, but Jane Yolen wrote a biography with a twist. She told their famous story from the point of view of their little sister, Katharine. And you would think that every aspect of George Washington's life has been dissected and discussed in every manner of book and article, but that's not true. Most kids were not familiar with his enthusiasm for farming until Peggy wrote *Farmer George Plants a Nation*. So find some aspect of a famous person's life that has settled in the shadows, and shine your biographical flashlight on it.

> Biographies are not limited to heroes and achievers. Books are also written about notorious rascals and traitors . . . and ordinary folks who did extraordinary things in the face of adversity.

But biographies are not limited to heroes and achievers. Books are also written about notorious rascals and traitors. James Giblin admits he doesn't always choose characters he admires, having written about Adolf Hitler, John Wilkes Booth, and Senator Joe McCarthy. He didn't like everything that Thomas Jefferson stood for, nor Charles A. Lindbergh's ties to the Nazi regime. "But," he says, "I felt these men were worth writing about because their actions made a lasting impact on human history. Consequently, I think it is important for young people to know about them, if only—as in the case of Hitler—to be on guard against similarly dangerous leaders who may arise in the future."

Ordinary folks who did extraordinary things in the face of adversity are also popular subjects for biographies. "Unsung people are always great to discover," says John Riley, founder and editor of young adult nonfiction publisher Morgan Reynolds. He has published biographies about little-known botanist and adventurer Ynes Mexia, and an obscure revolutionary named Vaclav Havel who instigated the fall of communism. The underlying issue, Riley says, is the importance of the person's contribution to his or her field.

Much has been written about the Holocaust and the horrors of World War II, but each year more amazing stories are uncovered. David Adler's biography titled *A Hero and the Holocaust* tells the story of Janusz Korczak, who was the director of a Jewish orphanage in Warsaw, Poland. He could have saved his own life but he stood by the children under his care, marching with them into the ghettos, then into the cattle cars, and then to the Treblinka death camp. And in the picture book, *Music for the End of Time*, author Jen Bryant wrote about French composer Olivier Messiaen, who was detained in a German prison camp during World War II. He missed his family and his home, of course, but he missed music even more. But as the book jacket says, "a chance encounter with a nightingale and a German officer provides Olivier with a small miracle—the opportunity to write music again."

When searching for a person to write about, consult magazine theme lists, find out what major historic anniversaries are approaching, and ask teachers for their advice. Who would they like to know more about? When Peggy asked Suzanne Shearman what the students at Barclay Elementary needed, the library media specialist simply waved her hand over the entire biography section and said, "More. We need more books about people kids haven't heard about yet."

Elements of Biography

Writing a biography is similar to writing about any other topic, but there are a few areas of special concern. Where does your person's story begin? How do you ground the character in reality? And how should you handle the negative as well as positive aspects of someone's personality or activities?

Beginnings

"A good biography for young readers needs to have a hook chapter that will make the child want to keep reading," says David Dilkes, Managing Editor at Enslow. "I guarantee you the youngster is more likely to check out or purchase the book that starts with an exciting scene or anecdote [rather] than background information." That is great advice, but *when* do you start?

Most children's biographies tend to be chronological. Young readers think in a linear progression and prefer biographies that start at the beginning of a person's life and move forward to the end. Children's biographies may also include more of the person's childhood, which makes for a strong connection between the subject and the reader. But that doesn't mean that you must start from day one unless the circumstances of that moment will shed light on the life that follows. Perhaps the most unusual birth documented on the first page of a children's book is in *The Trouble Begins at 8*. Newbery medalist Sid Fleischman wrote:

> Most children's biographies tend to be chronological . . . but that doesn't mean that you must start from day one.

> Mark Twain was born fully grown, with a cheap cigar clamped between his teeth.
>
> The event took place, as far as is known, in a San Francisco hotel room sometime in the fall of 1865. The only person attending was a young newspaperman and frontier jester named Samuel Langhorne Clemens.

Is there an event in your character's childhood that foreshadows the key characteristics that will become your focus, or reveals an inner conflict that recurs later on? Look how effectively Janice Tingum uses this childhood scene to introduce the biography of E. B. White:

> Elwyn ran to the stable the moment he heard that the eggs were

hatching. Fifty eggs, to be exact. He could hear the tiny beaks pecking against the eggshells as he approached the warming tray.

When the pecking finally stopped, all the eggs had hatched, except three. The family's coachman declared the three eggs worthless and disposed of them, unbroken, in a manure pile outside.

After a while, Elwyn heard a distant peeping sound. Running outside to investigate, he found three newly hatched chicks in the manure pile.

Many years later, in 1952, Elwyn Brooks White wrote *Charlotte's Web*, about a pig named Wilbur whose friend rescues him from death. By telling that true story, this biographer was able to show readers E. B. White's life-long awe and respect for nature, and also the genesis of his most famous book.

Carol Reed-Jones begins the biography *Hildegard of Bingen: Woman of Vision*, with the moment it became clear that Hildegard was special. The five-year-old described to her nurse the calf inside a pregnant cow. When the calf was born, the nurse was astonished to see that the markings were just as Hildegard said they would be. Before readers turn the first page, they know they are going to read about a very unusual character.

Another effective lead is to show a major event in the person's adult years, something related to why the person is noteworthy. Biographer Barbara Kramer begins her biography of John Glenn with the liftoff of *Friendship 7* in 1962, to introduce him and his claim to fame. In Chapter Two she goes back in time to discuss his childhood. For older children a flashback is easy to follow. Kathleen Krull starts her biography of Houdini with a scene from one of his acts in 1908, and then seamlessly flashes back to his birth in 1874.

For characters who may not be household names, showing them at work gives a better sense of their career. For example, the biography of motocross champion Ricky Carmichael begins with him revving his Honda CR250R at the starting line of a race.

David Adler begins his biography of Janusz Korczak by foreshadowing the conflict to come. "In Europe, 1878 was a year of Great Promise. In Rome, a new pope was chosen. A new king was crowned . . . But in 1878, there was a hint, too, of coming tragedy. In Gotha, Germany, Europe's first crematorium was built for use at funerals." That is a chilling opening but it sets the stage perfectly.

Play around with different leads to find the best way to introduce your subject and set up the mind story or narrative thread that will illuminate the person's life and achievements.

Ground Your Character in the Real World

A weak biography creates the false impression that the subject lived separate from the world, floating around in space. In all the biographies by Jean Fritz, Russell Freedman, Sid Fleischman, and James Giblin, among others, readers almost feel as though they are reading novels because they hear conversations, and see the action and the settings that make people come alive.

Grounding a biography in the reality of the times shows the reader how environment, traditions, and culture shaped a person's life. For example, in *When Marian Sang*, author Pam Muñoz Ryan thought it was important to show opera star Marian Anderson riding in the colored-only train cars and singing to two separate audiences, one black and one white. That was the world Anderson had to struggle through to become the first black woman to sing with the Metropolitan Opera.

> Grounding a biography in the reality of the times shows the reader how environment, traditions, and culture shaped a person's life.

When researching your character, gather basic biographical information (hometown, family, schooling, job) as well as information about his or her surroundings and environment. What was going on in the world at the same time? Such details will show your readers what the subject's life was like, and help explain decisions made and actions taken. Although

Peggy's biography of George Washington narrowed in on his farming, it was also important to use a wider lens to show the conflict between Great Britain and the colonies. Washington changed his farming techniques because of the exorbitant taxes that eventually led to colonial outrage and the Revolutionary War. He had already successfully separated Mount Vernon from the British economy and knew that he would have to help the colonies do the same. If he had not experienced the difficulties as a landowner, he might not have been compelled to lead the fight.

Warts and All

Along with grounding your subject in the real world, you also have to paint a picture of him or her that is so clear you could recognize the person on the street. This description is not the police blotter five-foot-two, blonde hair, blue eyes portrait, but something real.

Russell Freedman opens *Lincoln* with these lines: "Abraham Lincoln wasn't the sort of man who could lose himself in a crowd. After all, he stood six feet tall, and to top it off, he wore a high silk hat. His height was mostly in his long bony legs. It was only when he stood up that he towered above the other men. At first glance, most people thought he was homely."

> Don't be afraid to show your subject as a real human being with flaws and foibles.

A few paragraphs later, Freedman lets us see Lincoln's expression change as he begins to speak. "'The dull, listless features dropped like a mask,' wrote a Chicago newspaperman. 'The eyes began to sparkle, the mouth to smile, the whole countenance was wreathed in animation, so that a stranger would have said, "Why this man, so angular and solemn a moment ago, is really handsome".'" All through the book, Freedman shows Lincoln in different situations in a way that is never condescending or trivial.

Don't be afraid to show your subject as a real human being with flaws and foibles. Ben Rosenthal, Editor at Enslow, wants a biography that displays the subject's humanity and what that person was really like. Einstein becomes more accessible when we know that he was a terrible student. When bored, Einstein disrupted class and was disrespectful to the teacher. Lindbergh was an admirer of and a frequent visitor to Germany before and during WWII and spoke publicly against America's involvement in the war.

In the same respect, you must also show the human side of someone as notorious as Adolf Hitler. As a young artist, he loved his mother so much that he devoted all his time to caring for her on her deathbed. Does this garner him sympathy? No, but it completes a picture of a real human being. "Writers walk a tightrope in attempting to portray a destructive figure like Hitler," Giblin says. "There is always the temptation to resort to labels, defining the person as evil from the start. But that doesn't help readers to gain a clearer understanding of how he or she got that way." In his biographies, Giblin lets the action unfold. For example, he shows Hitler making his plans to conquer Europe and wipe out Jews. "I hope they [the readers] will *feel* the evil nature of Hitler's deeds without my having to spell it out."

> Include anecdotes that are humorous and tragic, as well as triumphant.

Kids need to know that even the most respected people goofed up, had bad moods, bad tempers, or bad habits. The subtext lets kids know that they too can achieve greatness despite their mistakes. So include anecdotes that are humorous and tragic, as well as triumphant. In her biography of Elizabeth Cady Stanton, author Deborah Kent told the story of how the suffragette cured her sons of cursing at the dinner table. Stanton invited several prominent friends one evening and they cursed throughout the meal. Her sons were so embarrassed that they promised to stop swearing if she did. Including a funny story like this reminds children that an otherwise solemn-looking figure in a faded black-and-white photo was a real person with emotions and a sense of humor.

Picture Book Biographies

Biographies for five- to eight-year-olds are usually tightly focused and about characters children are familiar with. Chances are good that your subject may already have a biography on library shelves, but even picture book biographies about the same person can still be very different.

Consider these four picture books about Abraham Lincoln and how each author wrote about a different aspect of Lincoln's life: Kay Winters zeroes in on Lincoln's love of learning despite his rustic upbringing in *Abe Lincoln: The Boy Who Loved Books*. Kathleen Krull highlights Lincoln's humor in *Lincoln Tells a Joke: How Laughter Saved the President (and the Country)*. *Abe Lincoln Goes to Washington*, by Cheryl Harness, focuses on Lincoln's professional years from 1837 to 1865, when he was a lawyer in Springfield, Illinois, through his presidency and the Civil War. And Ann Turner's biography takes a more unusual perspective: *Abe Lincoln Remembers* covers the major events in Lincoln's life through flashbacks, as Lincoln sits and waits for his wife to get dressed for the theater.

Paring down a picture book biography is difficult because there will be a lot of wonderful information left on the cutting room floor when you are done, and you will have to have fortitude to leave it there. Just remind yourself that your biography will be stronger with a tighter focus. You can use those leftovers in a sidebar, or another article or two. And remember that young children have a narrow vocabulary and a limited worldview. But editors warn: Don't condescend. Don't shy away from difficult concepts. Do your best to communicate complex ideas in a way that children can understand.

> Paring down a picture book biography is difficult because there will be a lot of information left on the cutting room floor when you are done, and you will have to have fortitude to leave it there.

Take advantage of your choice of words and writing style to reflect the subject's life. Carole Boston Weatherford writes *I, Matthew Henson* in first person to great effect. "I did not walk forty miles from the nation's capital to Baltimore's busy harbor to eye ships from a dock . . ." We hear the determination that propelled this explorer all the way to the North Pole.

In *We Are the Ship*, Kadir Nelson chose to narrate the story of the Negro Baseball League with the voice of a retired player reflecting on the good old days. "Seems like we've been playing baseball for a mighty long time . . ."

A poetic voice may paint a life of struggle and victory as it does in *When Marian Sang*. "It was her range of notes that caused all the commotion," writes Pam Muñoz Ryan. "With one breath she sounded like rain, sprinkling high notes in the morning sun. And with the next she was thunder, resounding deep in the dark sky." Ryan even weaves in song lyrics that echo changing moods.

> Listen closely to the voice of your character. Should he or she tell the story?

Other texts might benefit from being sparse and straightforward, reflecting a life that dealt with the world head on, as in the biography of artist Frida Kahlo. In *Frida*, Jonah Winter writes, "All of a sudden, Frida falls very ill. She's in bed for months. There's something wrong with one of her legs. Even her imaginary friend can't cheer her. That's when Frida teaches herself to draw. Drawing saves her from being sad."

So listen closely to the voice of your character. Should he or she tell the story? Jennifer Berne said yes when she wrote *Manfish: A Story of Jacques Cousteau*. Her elegant prose is reminiscent of Cousteau's narration of his undersea films.

Collective Biographies

A fun way to break into biographies is to collect the stories of more than one person with a common interest. My book, *Wild Animals, Gentle Women*, devotes one chapter each to ten women who studied and worked with animals.

At the time, Jane Goodall was just beginning to be recognized for her work in the Gombe with the chimpanzees. Dian Fossey, also in Africa, was studying gorillas, and Biruté Galdikas had just begun her work with orangutans in Borneo. Because these women were famous, it was easy to find information about them, and I was fortunate to be able to interview Jane Goodall in person. But I also wanted to include women who were less well known, or who were working with different animals. And that's where my fascination with old books paid off.

In a used bookstore, I found a battered copy of a book published in 1940, called *My Life in a Man-Made Jungle*, by Belle J. Benchley. She opened her story with these intriguing words: "If you can imagine yourself a middle-aged woman suddenly turned loose in a jungle of unknown creatures, because of the unexpected necessity of supporting yourself and a son of high-school age, you will have some idea of the consternation, to put it mildly, with which I found myself in the fall of 1925, embarked upon a career in the Zoological Garden of San Diego. I did not choose to work in a zoo. I was appointed to a job there by a Civil Service Commission. The position was that of a book-keeper . . ." As the world's first female zoo director, Belle Benchley became famous for displaying the first gorillas brought to the United States, and for nurturing young animals that were born in the zoo. Belle Benchley's story was the perfect opening for my book, and I went on to tell about other women in similar situations, some famous, others virtually unknown.

I interviewed Kay McKeever, who cares for owls at the Owl Foundation in Ontario, Canada, not far across the border from my home, and Hope Buyukmihci, who rescues beavers in New Jersey. My last chapter is called

"Is Animal Watching for You?" In it, I suggest ways to prepare for such careers, because that kind of information adds to the book's usefulness, especially in school libraries.

Women's history is a popular subject area for collective biographies. Laurie Halse Anderson's *Independent Dames*, Tanya Lee Stone's award-winning *Almost Astronauts*, Cheryl Harness's *Remember the Ladies*, and Julie Cummins's *Women Daredevils* are just a few. Stone hit upon her idea after reading a newspaper article that made a single reference to the group of women now referred to as the "Mercury 13." She was intrigued enough to want to find out more. Her research led her to enlightening primary source documents, original photos of the women, and even interviews with surviving members of the group.

A strong collection should contain a wide variety of stories and people. Look for the famous and the obscure, the uplifting and the tragic. Kathleen Krull's *Lives of the Writers* offers lively biographical sketches of literary luminaries; Phillip Hoose's *We Were There, Too!* highlights dozens of young people who played a role in events that shaped America; and William O'Malley's *Dare to Dream* tells the stories of 16 ordinary people who became *somebodies*. Be selective. Ask yourself, "Is this person's story compelling? What challenges did each one face? How can their stories teach or motivate readers?"

Contemporary Profiles and Biographies

So far we have only talked about historical biographies. But young people are fascinated by current sports figures, rock stars, and movie idols, as well as children their own age with unusual stories to tell. "Even if a child doesn't like to read, if he or she loves a certain celeb, he or she is more likely to pick up the book," says Joanne Mattern, who has written biographies on many famous people including Michelle Obama, the Jonas Brothers, and Lebron James.

Writing a biography of someone who is still alive may sound

intimidating. What if your subject does not like what you write? That should not be a concern if you are confident in your research skills. In order to minimize any negative comments, Barbara Kramer, author of several contemporary biographies, says, "I use a lot of sources, and I keep careful records of them so I can back up what I've written." She is also careful about her subjects, choosing people she admires with upstanding character.

> To find a good subject for your biography, read the newspaper, watch TV, or listen to the kids at the bus stop to find out who they are talking about and what the latest craze is.

To find a good subject for your biography, read the newspaper, watch TV, or listen to the kids at the bus stop to find out who they are talking about and what the latest craze is. Once people reach celebrity status, anyone can write about them. You don't need their permission to write an "unauthorized" biography. If the subject you choose is not a celebrity, you will need to get permission to interview him or her. Q. L. Pearce, who has written several biographies for KidHaven's Young Heroes series, says, "Be prepared to tell the subject how you will structure the story. A person will probably be more willing to cooperate if they feel comfortable with the approach."

The research process is the same as it would be for any other topic. First look at other books and articles in print. Two library references to consult are *Current Biography* and *Biography Today*, which provide brief bios of people in the news, from political figures to professional athletes. Each article gives a general overview of the person's life and achievements, and lists additional references to consult, including a contact person such as an agent or public relations firm.

Contact your subject directly or through an agent or publicist if necessary. Say that you are writing a children's book or article and would like an interview. The celebrity may be too busy to talk with you, but you may be able to ask questions using the agent as an intermediary; at the very least you have alerted the person of your intentions. A lesser-known individual will be more likely to agree to an interview, so prepare a list of questions that, as Pearce points out, "when answered, give you not only information but insight. You want to get a sense of the subject's character."

Pearce writes about contemporary youngsters like Hannah Taylor, an 11-year-old Canadian who founded an organization to help the homeless, and Given Kachepa, who fights against human trafficking. Interviews are an important part of her research process. "I can ask quirky questions that I know will interest my readers. The quotes are fresh and I get a real sense of the subject's personality. If I need to confirm something that I have read about them, I simply email and ask." In the interviews, Pearce asks about hobbies, school, and plans for the future to show that her subjects are typical kids. "That's what makes each of these young people such great role models. They are kids with homework and household chores. They like pizza, music, movies, and hanging out with their friends. These everyday elements are the framework when I write about the extraordinary things these children have accomplished."

Pearce feels that writing about current personalities who are willing to be interviewed is faster than writing historical biographies, and presents fewer research issues. It should be easier to find accurate sources, with fewer gaps in the information. Still, according to Joanne Mattern, you have to stay on top of current events when writing about a person whose life is continually changing. "They go on living while you're writing, which can really mess up your research!" In her biography of Tom Cruise, Mattern wrote about his marriage to Nicole Kidman, whom he was still married to at the time. Shortly after the book went to press, Cruise announced their divorce, but it was too late to update the book. For Mattern, it was discouraging to have her book become obsolete so quickly, but it is an unavoidable hazard with living subjects.

Another concern is how to end a person's story when they continue to live, work, or create. Keep it open-ended, suggests Pearce, or as Mattern notes, "inspiring yet vague." She adds, "It's usually appropriate to say that the subject will face more triumphs and challenges in the future."

Biography Websites

If you are looking for information about a particular person or just want to browse, here are a few online sources to check out:

Academy of Achievement: www.achievement.org
This site offers contemporary biographies, profiles, and interviews with people in business, the arts, sports, science, and public service.

Distinguished Women of Past and Present: www.distinguishedwomen.com
This site has biographies of women who contributed to American culture in many different ways: writers, educators, scientists, heads of state, politicians, civil rights crusaders, artists, entertainers, and others.

Heritage Gateways: http://heritage.uen.org/
An interesting site to gather biographical information about pioneers. It includes diary excerpts and other first-person accounts.

Innovative Lives: www.invention.smithsonian.org
This website comes from the Lemelson Center for the Study of Invention and Innovation, which is part of the Smithsonian. It lists dozens of fascinating inventions and inventors.

My Hero: http://myhero.com
An inspiring website that features the achievements of people from all walks of life. The directory includes categories such as Earth keepers, lifesavers, and angels.

4000 Years of Women in Science: www.astr.ua.edu/4000WS
You can search through lists chronologically or by subject to find bios, sometimes brief, of women from ancient Greece to today who advanced our scientific knowledge.

Contemporary Magazine Profiles

A magazine profile is a short biography with a narrower focus than a book. For example, rather than covering Johnny Depp's entire life, a profile may highlight his work in a particular film. The tight theme helps to structure the article, naturally creating a logical beginning and conclusion.

A magazine profile is the perfect vehicle to showcase someone who may not grace the cover of *Time*, but whose work can inspire young readers. Many magazines such as *Next Step*, *Cricket*, and *Insight* welcome profiles of people who have overcome struggles or in some way changed the world for the better. For example, *Boys' Life* has published profiles of people who keep waterways clean, *Yes Mag* has featured scientists who work in the Arctic, and the Canadian publication, *KNOW*, published a profile of Dorothy Harrison Eustis, a guide dog trainer.

If a magazine has a theme, think of people who might fit into that particular category. For example, an issue about birds might publish a profile of a bird breeder, a raptor rehabilitator, the director of an aviary, an ornithologist, or a wildlife artist who specializes in illustrating birds. Think out of the box, and try to make connections between what appear to be very different areas. For example, profiling a real-life adventurer could yield an interesting angle on a storytelling theme, and an article on a scientist who uses math to predict hurricanes would be welcomed by an editor working on an issue about natural disasters. Editor Lynn Gilliam of *Pockets* advises writers to identify "the first thing you think of when you think of that theme—and don't write about that!" Her advice applies to profiles and just about any other kind of article.

Markets for profiles abound, as they do for biographies, and the possibilities for subjects are endless. Regional and local magazines and newspapers are an excellent place to begin practicing your biography writing skills and gain entry into the writing market.

Chapter 8

Dissecting Science and Nature Writing

Finding Your Focus

The Human Element

Thinking Like a Child

Making It Accessible

"All I hope to say in books, all that I ever hope to say, is that I love the world."

—E. B. White, author of *Charlotte's Web*

C hildren innately grow up curious. They are natural little scientists, experimenting and learning about the world around them. But some-where on the path to adulthood many kids develop an unnatural view of Earth. We agree with Sy Montgomery's observation that many kids tend to think of the real world as steel and concrete, money, cars, and shopping. It is every science and nature writer's ambition to remind children that the real world is better than that. It is green and blue, gooey and glorious, and pulsing with life.

Adrienne Mason, editor of *KNOW* magazine, acknowledges the com-plexity of this task. "In my estimation," she says, "[science and nature writing] is one of the most difficult genres because you need to be simple, clear, engaging, *and* scientifically accurate." It can be hard at times, but it is so rewarding. There are many wonderful tales to tell and kids love to hear them. The natural history of an animal, plant, or microbe is one kind of narrative, but there are also stories behind every scientific fact and discovery. All it takes to write about science and nature for children is the ability to make the topic accessible to a young reader, and to find the *people* behind the science.

The Human Element

Award-winning science writer David Quammen says, "Science, like democracy, tai chi, and golf, is a human activity. It's not a body of truth. Science is a subject of humanity." William Zinsser agrees. "You can take much of the mystery out of science writing," he says, "by helping readers to identify with the scientific work being done. This means looking for the human element."

> Let kids see that science is not a body of facts etched in stone, but ever-changing ideas that shift with the tide of technology.

You and your reader can become the human element that Quammen and Zinsser speak of, but you can also show the paths that scientists have taken, the patterns of scientific research, and the stories behind it all. Let kids see that science is not a body of facts etched in stone, but ever-changing ideas that shift with the tide of technology.

The Story Behind Discovery

Here is a *fact*: Alexander Fleming discovered penicillin in 1928. But in *Healing Drugs*, I go beyond that fact to tell the *story* surrounding one of the most amazing examples of human ingenuity and perseverance known to science.

Although Fleming *discovered* penicillin, he could not interest the rest of the medical community in his discovery so he filed away his notes, where they sat for ten years until Howard Walter Florey and Ernst Boris Chain rediscovered them. At that time, England was gearing up for World War II and there was no money for research, but Florey and Chain knew that if penicillin could be produced in large quantities it could save soldiers' lives. They grew the penicillin mold Fleming described in his papers in every available pie pan, china platter, letterbox, and hospital bedpan. Threats of a German invasion prompted the researchers to protect the priceless penicillin mold by rubbing spores into the pockets of their suits and the linings of their rain-coats. During a blitz, hopefully one scientist could carry the mold to safety.

The first patient to receive penicillin was an Oxford policeman dying from a small, infected scratch. Penicillin was dripped into his veins, but was quickly excreted with his urine. Florey and Chain's wives formed a "P-patrol" to collect the urine and bicycle it over to the lab so the penicillin could be extracted. The policeman recovered within 24 hours. But the meager supply of penicillin ran out, and he died a month later. Shortly after, a 14-year-old boy was treated and survived. For the first time the words "miracle drug" were used. But still no pharmaceutical company would produce it.

The scientists were just about to give up when Japan attacked Pearl Harbor. Ten days later in an unprecedented unified effort, four major drug companies joined forces to produce penicillin for American troops, and the U.S. government ordered military personnel to collect soil samples from around the world in the hopes of discovering another potential miracle mold. But it wasn't until Mary Hunt found a moldy cantaloupe in the trash that a better antibiotic was made. Her discovery earned her the nickname "Moldy Mary."

> You might forget the dates and names, but once you read about Florey's moldy pockets, the P-patrol, and Moldy Mary, you'll never forget the struggle behind the discovery of penicillin.

You might forget the dates and names, but once you read about Florey's moldy pockets, the P-patrol, and Moldy Mary, you'll never forget the struggle behind the discovery of penicillin. That is the human element.

In *What's the Buzz?* I tell the story of David Roubik and James Nich as they devised experiments to figure out how stingless bees communicate, from setting up a colony, to labeling and training each bee, designing special feeders, and recording bee buzz. Readers can follow along as the researchers ask new questions and figure out ways to get answers, allowing readers to see for themselves the mix-ups, the failures, and the successes. But it is not just the science that I present. I include information about what it's like to live at the research station and canoe to the research site, work in the dark wearing night goggles, and climb to the top of the rain forest canopy.

Sometimes a book is a compilation of smaller anecdotes that, presented together, provide a full history of a field of science. Peggy uses this format in *Medicines from Nature*, where she features the research of entomologist Thomas Eisner, ethnobotanist Mark Plotkin, and the National Cancer Institute, among others. A single anecdote, on the other hand, can fill the need of magazines like *Odyssey*, *Dig*, *Ask*, *National Geographic Kids*, or *Highlights*, whose editors are always looking for articles that show scientists as they work. In Cynthia Graber's article "Sea Turtle Saver," published in *Ranger Rick*, she describes how Wallace J. Nichols monitors and protects sea turtles in Baja, California. Graber not only describes the science, but also Nichols's work with local fisherman and governments to change long-held attitudes regarding the sea turtle.

Get Involved

Like most science and nature writers, we like to get involved with our subjects. We have already mentioned eating insects, and working the night shift on a research vessel, but we've also counted birds, taken weather measurements, and excavated mastodons to bring a personal touch to our writing. Award-winning author Sy Montgomery has turned this strategy into a fine art with her series Scientists in the Field. With photographer Nic Bishop, Montgomery has followed scientists as they study snow leopards, parrots, tree kangaroos, bears, and tarantulas. In *Saving the Ghost of the*

Mountain, Montgomery puts herself in the narrative, introducing the team members and locals she met, describing the exhausting hikes along mountain ledges, the frustration of not seeing a snow leopard, and the bizarre thrill of finding scat: "As if he's savoring some special cheese or fine wine, Tom [the researcher] picks up the poop and sniffs it." Because Montgomery invests herself in the project she is able to hook her reader, who instantly thinks, "Wow, I wonder if I could do that."

Any research trip, even one to Mongolia, starts with a simple phone call.

You might be asking yourself the same thing. And the answer is yes. Montgomery, a naturalist in her own right and the author of dozens of books for children and adults, has clout that you may not have yet acquired, but just remember that any research trip, even one to Mongolia, starts with a simple phone call. My research trip all those years ago to the Galapagos would not have happened had I not called Richard T. Barber at Duke University's Marine Lab. Start small. Contact the people in your area who are doing research or conservation work and see if you can lend a hand.

You don't have to be part of a team either. You can experience science and nature in your own backyard. As Jim Arnosky notes in *Secrets of a Wildlife Watcher*, "Wherever you go there is wildlife to watch. Even in the largest cities, squirrels are sharing trees with bats, songbirds, and owls. There are pigeons nesting on ledges. Spiders design webs in windows and mice crisscross floors." Step outside and observe the life around you. Lie on your belly and study the grass, spend a night under the stars. Experiment, too. Keep a magnifying glass, binoculars, and notebook by the door so when you find an interesting insect or an odd bird behavior you can use your own words to describe it. You can communicate more effectively what you have seen with your own eyes, heard with your own ears, and felt with your own hands, than you can if you only report it in the third person. Share the sensations and emotions with your reader. Coupled with solid research you'll create an accessible true story.

Facklam Files:
Peggy's Thoughts on the Amazon

Over the summer I boarded a boat, along with my mother and sister-in-law Terry, that took us down the Peruvian Amazon. Each morning the sun quickly heated the air and warmed the giant moths and beetles that had hitched a midnight ride on our windowsill. And each night we hustled into our cabin, safe from the thick swarms of mosquitoes. In between we spied sleeping sloths in the rain forest canopy, fished for piranhas and ate our catch, visited thatched-hut villages, and were blessed by a shaman. It was an experience that sparked so many ideas that my notebook brims with sketches, notes, quotes from our guide, questions, and impressions. Each photo brings back a flood of memories of the animals we encountered and the people we met.

What surprises me most is that I haven't yet published anything about the trip. I have recorded my thoughts, but my focus is not clear. I seem to need a little more distance from an experience before I can envision the structure of the story I want to tell. Of all the ideas I have, which one will come to the surface first? I know I will eventually write about the buttressed trees, the hanging lianas, and the mysterious pink dolphins. I'm just not done soaking it all in.

Plus, I am still doing research. Personal experience is great, but it needs to be bolstered by old-fashioned bookwork. The information that I hastily scribbled in my notebook needs to be fact-checked. Does the Amazon River really discharge enough water into the ocean in one hour to drown out an area the size of France to a depth of 43 feet? And I need to research the market too. In the last few years, has any magazine published the legend of the Amazon?

When I do write about it, my notebook will be the palette from which I can draw those vivid images. "Thursday—6:00am—Mist hangs low over the river and shoreline. As the sun rises, the sky blushes briefly. Morning doesn't linger here (neither does sunset) . . . This morning we hear a flock of parakeets, clattering away at the top of several Cecropia trees, sounding like a late-night party spilling out onto the early morning sidewalk." Even if I never publish a word about the Amazon, I know that those experiences and those memories have not only enriched my writing, but also my soul.

Invite Your Reader In

Make your reader the human element. Create a connection between your subject and your reader's life. Faith McNulty uses the second person pronoun 'you' as she shows what it would be like *If You Decide to Go to the Moon.* I used this approach when writing *Bugs for Lunch.* Because the ending of this nonfiction picture book shows children from other cultures eating insects, I wanted to tap into readers' imaginations right from the start. By the time they turned the last page, I wanted kids to imagine themselves happily eating a roasted witchetty grub. So my first page reads:

> If your lunch was a bug,
> Who could you be?
> Maybe a nuthatch
> at work in a tree.

Susan E. Goodman applies the same technique in *Claws, Coats and Camouflage.* By asking right at the beginning, "What would happen if you pulled a goldfish out of its bowl to play video games?" Goodman connects with readers so they will understand that the concept of adaptation applies to humans as well. The paragraph finishes with: "It would be in big trouble. Then again, you would be too if you went underwater without bringing any air along."

Another way to connect is to give readers something to do. Kids are active. They like to participate. Visit an elementary school and you'll find a classroom with a pet tarantula, another with a snake, turtle, rabbit, or guinea pig. Or you'll see kids busy with projects to plant trees or clean up their schoolyard. Many adults hold science at arms' length as if it is not a part of their lives, but science and nature beg kids to jump in, get dirty, and have fun, so give them a quick activity to do within the text. Seymour Simon engages the reader right away in *The Heart.* "Make a fist," he says. "This is about the size of your heart." You'll be pleasantly surprised to know that kids actually follow directions. While working at the public library, Peggy witnessed many children holding a fist up to their chest. In

The Kids' World Almanac of Amazing Facts About Numbers, Math and Money, Peggy and I invite readers to do all sorts of things including plot the longitude and latitude of their hometown, take their pulse, and decipher a code.

Include a sidebar or a section at the back with a recipe or experiment. Jim Arnosky adds directions on how to collect aquatic insects in the back of *The Brook Book: Exploring the Smallest Streams*, and there is an entire page of activities in *Whose Idea Was That? Inventions That Changed Our Lives* by David Ellyard.

You can even engage older kids. Dana Meachen Rau's book, *Alternative Energy: Beyond Fossil Fuels*, is a conversation with young adult readers that asks questions and makes them think. She also encourages kids to calculate their carbon footprint and become part of the discussion on the energy sources they will use in the future.

Writing Accessible Science

Richard Feynman was a physicist who won the Nobel Prize in 1965 for his brilliant discoveries. In his book, *The Pleasure of Finding Things Out*, he described how, on walks through the woods, his dad would spot a bird and ask, "Do you know what bird that is? It's a brown-throated thrush; but in Portuguese it's a . . . In Italian it's a . . . In Chinese it's a . . . etc." Then he'd say, "You know in all the languages what the name of that bird is, and when you've finished with that, you'll know absolutely nothing whatever about the bird. Now, let's look at the bird." Feynman said, "He taught me to notice things. That's the way I was educated . . . with those kinds of examples and discussion, no pressure, just lovely, interesting discussions."

"He taught me to notice things. That's the way I was educated . . . with those kinds of examples and discussion, no pressure, just lovely, interesting discussions."

And that's how you write about science for children or adults: "No pressure, just lovely, interesting discussions." You should write about ants the same way you would explain ants to a small child while lying on your bellies watching the endless six-legged parade march across the sidewalk in front of your house. Don't be cutesy, but matter-of-fact and honest. Use a conversational voice as you translate the scientific facts into a true story. Two common mistakes that editors encounter are writers who write over the heads of the readers using the language of an academic, or talking down to readers, sounding like a simpering aging auntie.

To strike that balance in children's nonfiction you need to do three things: 1) Find your focus. 2) Know your audience. 3) Think like a child.

And remember, you don't need to have a science degree to write about science. Editors are looking for writers who have the ability to dig for facts and weave those facts into a good story. In his book *Levitating Trains and Kamikaze Genes*, Richard Brennan said, "One of the challenges of good science writing is striking the right balance between general and detailed. Scientists and engineers often write books that are too technical by far for general readers. Journalists, on the other hand, often write material that is too superficial. Balance is the goal here." To strike that balance in children's nonfiction you need to do three things: 1) Find your focus. 2) Know your audience. 3) Think like a child.

Find Your Focus

Most magazine editors do not want a general overview about a branch of science or the entire natural history of an animal species. *Highlights for Children* mentions in its contributor's guidelines that, "Articles with a tight focus are more successful." In other words, write in manageable bits. Rather than an article about the ocean or outer space, write about riptides or the space station. Instead of writing about the natural history of the gecko, focus on one aspect of the animal—its sticky toes, for example. Look at several children's magazines and study the kinds of articles inside. Consider how they may have been narrowed down from a larger topic. For the science magazine *Odyssey*, Betty J. Pfeiffer's article, "The CIA Wants You: The Science and Art of Food Preparation," focuses specifically on the chemistry behind food preparation. *Young Rider*, a horse magazine, features articles on very specific aspects of horses and horse-riding; a typical issue might include an article about summer camp horses and another about teaching your horse to back up. Picture books tend to look through a narrow lens also. *The Big Bug Book* focused on size, while *Spiders and Their Web Sites* highlighted unusual web-builders.

Find your focus through preliminary research. Often while you are ferreting out information, a story will pop out and guide your thesis, but if it doesn't, ask a few questions. What is the most kid-friendly aspect of your topic? For example, if my general theme is chemistry, I would immediately think about the chemistry of smell. Kids love the gross factor. Or perhaps I'd look into how chemistry has improved sports equipment, or if it has any relationship to the little lights that flash on kids' sneakers.

If that doesn't work for you, then ask yourself: Is there a connection to current events? It is no coincidence that shortly after a natural disaster related articles appear in every periodical. Kids as well as adults like to read about what's happening in the world around them, and an article will be more appealing to an editor if you can tie it in to hot news. Author Andrew Klein realized that the recent blooms of jellyfish along the California coast was a good reason to write "Attack of the Jellyfish" for *Science World*, so he could help explain the phenomena and showcase the scientists studying jellyfish.

Keeping current also means finding out what is going on in labs right now. One of the finest science magazines for kids, *Odyssey*, specifies in its writer's guidelines that, "The inclusion of primary research (interviews with scientists focusing on current research) is of primary interest to the magazine." It has published stories on NASA's Cassini Equinox mission to photograph the moons Enceladus and Titan; how the American Red Cross keeps our blood supply safe; and cutting-edge technology in transportation. For the most recent updates, scope out news sources such as *Science Daily* or *Science News*, and drop in on national and international science association websites. That is how Peggy first heard about an animal study that she included in the final chapter of *Post Traumatic Stress Disorder*.

Odd-Ologies

Consider the familiar and the unfamiliar when looking for ideas. Here are a few fields of study that might pique your interest:

Anemology—the study of wind
Caliology—the study of bird's nests
Campanology—the study of bell ringing
Dysteleology—the study of purposeless organs
Oology—the study of eggs
Pelology—the study of mud
Scatology—the study of poop
Xylology—the study of wood

Know Your Audience

Children have a different way of looking at the world. They are literal yet imaginative, and you can tap into both of these abilities when you write about science and nature. Science for preschoolers can be as simple as learning shapes, colors, and the names of animals. Science for elementary kids is a big step up because they've been exposed to a huge range of subjects in class—especially involving animals—and on television. It's fun to write for older children because you can dig deeper and explain even more.

My editor presented me with a challenge one day when she asked me to write nonfiction for preschoolers. I had been writing for middle-grade readers as well as high school students, so I wasn't certain that I could do it. Writing short is hard. Every word must say exactly what you mean.

My first preschool lift-the-flap book, *So Can I*, has 77 words and compares things animals do with what a child can do. For example:

> A fish can swim.
> > So can I.
> A monkey can swing.
> > So can I.

The last page is the surprise:

> A bird can fly.
> > So can I.
> > But I need a little help!

The illustration shows children "flying" in an airplane carnival ride. Is that science? Not to an adult or a teenager, of course. But it may be a child's first look at comparisons, differences, and similarities. And it's fun.

You can write about almost any subject for any level of reader. We examined dozens of books to see how authors wrote about dinosaurs. For example, *Dinosaurs* by Gail Gibbons is a primer geared toward three- to eight-year-olds. It has minimal text, one to two sentences per page, and unfamiliar words, like *paleontologist*, are defined within the illustrations. In *Boy, Were We Wrong About Dinosaurs*, Kathleen Kudlinski builds on the reader's knowledge and presents the idea that paleontology is ever-changing. What we once knew about dinosaurs is wrong and what we believe now might be corrected in years to come. My chapter book for middle-grade readers, *Tracking Dinosaurs in the Gobi,* digs deep into the history of paleontology in that region, from the first American explorer, Roy Chapman Andrews, to current research taking place along the fossil-rich Flaming Cliffs.

There are no hard-and-fast rules about what you can't put in a picture book and what you can put in a chapter book or vice versa. Some picture book authors have tackled such complex concepts as the geometry of size in *Just The Right Size: Why Big Animals Are Big and Little Animals Are Little*, by Nicola Davies, and the creation of the universe in *Older Than the Stars*, by Karen C. Fox, who uses two narratives to tell the story. Young children can listen to the simple cumulative verse:

> This is the gas in a giant puff
> that spun from the blocks
> that formed from the bits
> that were born in the bang
> when the world began.

While older children can read a fuller explanation on the same page:

> Soon the universe was a jumble of helium and hydrogen atoms.
> Over millions of years, gravity pulled the atoms together until they grew
> into enormous clouds that were the size of galaxies, or even bigger.

Many authors employ two levels of narrative to give young kids access to the story and at the same time fill the need of older students for more information. This style creates a nice balance, widens your readership, and reinforces learning. Think about visiting your local school. You can plant sunflower seeds with the sixth-grade class just as you can in the kindergarten classroom. But while you are sitting with your knees thrust up to your chin you'll probably tell the five-year-olds how the seeds need water and sunlight to grow. The sixth graders, however, will be able to answer your questions about chlorophyll and photosynthesis. It is the same activity, the same information, but different intensities.

To be successful writing for any age level, you also have to be aware of the linear progression of the material. Before you can explain DNA, for instance, you first need to show your reader what a cell looks like and what chromosomes are. Before the sunflower comes the seed and seedling. Build the information from the ground up, from simple to complex.

Super Science Sites

Accuracy in science reporting is key, so get your information directly from researchers. Here are just a few websites that can connect you with scientists. Don't forget your local college and university faculty, too.

American Chemical Society: www.chemistry.org
Features current news articles and a kids' page with activities and experiments.

American Museum of Natural History: www.amnh.org
Provides the names of dozens of AMNH scientists and their field of research, from paleontology to genetics.

Massachusetts Institute of Technology:
http://web.mit.edu/research/
Some of the most brilliant minds are hard at work at MIT. It is an excellent place to look for images and experts.

NASA: www.nasa.gov
Provides up-to-date news on space missions, biographies of astronauts, and even story ideas. It also provides you with the address and phone number of the newsroom so you can contact them with questions.

Science.gov: http://science.gov
This website has links to dozens of research facilities.

Smithsonian Institution: www.si.edu/research
Lists research centers, as well as links to its extensive library and archives that you can search online.

U.S. Geological Survey: www.usgs.gov
Includes an extensive list of current projects by state, and contacts for each region.

Think Like A Child

Believe it or not, sometimes it helps when you know very little about your subject because, like a child, you are forced to learn from the beginning. Ask the kinds of questions that kids would ask: "How did you find out about that chemical?" "Wasn't it scary when you went down into that deep cave?" "What does a manatee sound like?" or "Is a sea slug squishy?"

Take readers into the natural world with all their senses. Show the colors, textures, and smells that create the feeling of the swamp, the rain forest, the desert, or a city park. Don't clutter the story with too much background, but give readers a sense of place. In her book, *If You Decide to Go to the Moon*, Faith McNulty says the dust on the moon is like cake flour. You'd want to play in it. And Sy Montgomery dots *Kakapo Rescue* with sensory details like the sound of a doorbell outside a tent to signal the volunteers sleeping inside that a Kakapo has left her nest. Montgomery also describes the flightless parrot as smelling like honey, growling like a dog, booming like a bullfrog, and clanging like a cash register.

> Show the colors, textures, and smells that create the feeling of the swamp, the rain forest, the desert, or a city park.

Kids love to be grossed out, so go for it. Author Fiona Bayrock says, "Sure a giraffe has a long tongue, but tell kids the giraffe uses its tongue to clean its ears (*Ewww, gross!*) and you've hooked them into reading more." She does this to great effect in articles like "Slimy Mucus, Sticky Goo!" and "Fungus with a Fastball," and in her book, *Bubble Homes and Fish Farts*, when describing how herring release "Fast Repetitive Ticks" (FaRTs) to talk to one another.

Use kid-friendly comparisons, or as Bayrock calls them, "relevant references." I use relevant references especially when describing size. The goliath tarantula, for instance, is so big that if it sat in the center of a dinner plate, its feet would hang over the edge. That is an image kids can see right away. Saying that a blue whale weighs ten tons will not evoke a vivid picture in your reader's mind. But say that a blue whale weighs more than a train engine, or is as long as nine minivans, and a child can easily imagine the magnitude of the measurement.

Be kid-friendly when describing actions and processes too. In *Spiders and Their Web Sites* I had to explain how a spider molts, so I watched as a tarantula arduously tugged each leg out of its old skin. Instantly, I was reminded of pulling fingers out of a tight glove. It works for all ages. Dana Rau compares the dilemma of running out of energy sources to the reader running out of his favorite breakfast cereal.

> Being familiar with the tools, toys, and technology kids use today can make your references even more relevant.

Being familiar with the tools, toys, and technology kids use today can make your references even more relevant. Ten years ago, you might have said a frog was the size of a baseball or a child's fist. But today you can mention that a frog is the size of a cell phone. Don't worry if you're a bit of a technophobe. You can stick to the basics such as body parts, or compare something to the size of the book the reader is holding or the text on the page. For *The Big Bug Book* even the illustrations showed life-size insects in or near common household objects like a baseball bat, a doorknob, and a wrench.

When it comes to writing about nature and science we could go on and on, but suffice it to say that it is as fun as it is challenging. The fun is in the research and the challenge is to write exciting and revealing books and articles that will elicit the response, "Wow, is that really true?" "Tell me more," or even "How do they do that?"

Chapter 9

Handling the How-to Genre

Writing Instructions ----┐

The How-to Market

Cracking the Magazine Market

Writing Self-help ----┘

"How-to articles let you become a teacher, where you pass along your skills to a whole new generation. You're the master and they, the fascinated apprentice."
—Jan Fields, author of *Wellspring of Magic* and editor of *Kid Magazine Writers* e-zine

When Peggy and I first thought about creating a book on writing nonfiction for children, we struggled with how to do it. We had both given countless workshops and talks on the subject and coached aspiring writers for the Institute of Children's Literature, but there was so much to say. How could we show someone how to write? How do you tell a person how to do *anything*?

As any good teacher knows, you must present the information clearly and you have to make the learning fun—two key characteristics of the successful how-to. Think of the how-to format like a party invitation. It should make the event sound fun or no one will come, and you must provide clear directions so that your guests can find their way.

The fun starts with your idea. Choose a kid-friendly topic. Write about a subject that children are already interested in, and will get excited about and want to try. Peggy's Toffee Surprise (see sidebar p. 168) had the "yuck" factor working in its favor because children like gross and messy activities. Give them a chance to experiment with the unknown, create fanciful gifts, and build things they can use.

> Almost any topic has potential as long as you put the fun up front.

Study the how-to market for titles that suggest an idea for a different approach or a new technique. Craft diva Ellen Warwick has been successful targeting teen girls with books on how to dress up their jeans, make purses, and decorate their rooms. But try turning that around. Perhaps there is a market for a how-to on revamping a boy's room or building a tree house loft bed. Almost any topic has potential as long as you put the fun up front.

Catch your reader's attention with a captivating title or lead. These are just a few titles that caught our eye: *Math Doesn't Suck: How to Survive Middle School Math Without Losing Your Mind or Breaking a Nail*; *How to Fossilize Your Hamster and Other Amazing Experiments for the Armchair Scientist*; *How to Beat Your Dad at Chess*; and *Play Soccer Like a Pro*. These titles speak a kid's language, conjure up enticing images, and promise success.

Your lead needs to motivate your reader into action as well as introduce your topic. For example, in *Creepy Crafts for Boys and Ghouls*, Kate Ritchey reminds kids, "When October 31 rolls around, you'll want to be ready with lots of Halloween treats. With the help of this book, you can make gifts, decorations, and even some delicious Halloween food. So what are you waiting for? It's time to make some creepy crafts!" With a deadline looming, most readers will fly into action.

Once you have the reader's attention, keep the information clear with precise language and careful organization. What will children come away with when they are finished reading? Are they creating a piece of art or learning a new skill? Then lead them step-by-step to a successful conclusion.

Anything that your reader constructs or creates, you should have built too—several times. This might sound like a no-brainer, but it is important that you know every step is in the proper order. There is nothing worse than getting halfway through a set of instructions and then reading, "But first . . ." Writer Dana Rau says her office is often a clutter of experiments. "Making a compass, tying friendship bracelets, sewing quilts. When I experiment I work out the kinks and unclear or misleading directions through trial and error."

Carol Johmann, author of several hands-on activity books, suggests a three-pronged approach to developing written instructions. First she constructs the object and takes notes as she makes it. Then she crafts it a second time following her own notes and polishing them as she goes. The third time, she has children follow her written instructions, after which she revises again if necessary. This process might seem lengthy but it gives Johmann the confidence that her final set of directions is clear and easy to follow.

> Anything that your reader constructs or creates, you should have built too—several times.

Consider how best to organize the material to achieve your intended goal. Part of presenting the information in a clear manner comes from the effective use of formatting. Elements such as headings, bullet points, numbering, bold type, and other organizing features serve as road signs for the reader, creating a visual map for navigating through the material. Such elements may be enhanced or otherwise altered by the publisher during the publishing process, but working them into your original manuscript provides the foundation for a set of instructions that paves the way to a successful project.

Facklam Files:
Peggy Bakes with Bugs

When the editor of *Cricket* called to personally accept my article, "Bugs for Breakfast," he asked me if I could add a kid-friendly recipe to go along with it. I laughed at his joke, until I realized he was serious. And so I launched into creating a culinary how-to on this very unusual subject.

I set out to find a recipe that was easy for kids to make, but also appetizing enough for my family because they would be the taste-testers. I used *Entertaining with Insects* by Ronald L. Taylor and Barbara J. Carter as my guide into insect cookery. I knew I couldn't use the recipe for mushrooms stuffed with mealworms because most kids don't eat mushrooms. I nixed Beetle Sausage. It required too much chopping and frying in a hot skillet. And although Jumping Jubilee promised to "brighten up the end of your meal," I chose a recipe for toffee. Anything mixed with brown sugar, butter, and chocolate had to be good—even insects.

Using the book's recipe as a base, I eliminated the nuts and altered the amounts to make a smaller batch. Then I tromped to the pet store for the crucial ingredient. Feeling like an idiot, I asked for a cup of mealworms, not knowing how one purchased live insects. Did they come prepackaged or could I scoop them out of the bulk section? (FYI: They come prepackaged in little cartons that look like the old-fashioned Skippy cups of ice cream.) My readers would likely have similar questions, so I'd have to pass on this information to them, too.

With all of the ingredients out on the table I wrote down each step in order:

1. Separate mealworms from the bedding/packaging material. I tried several methods—blowing on it works, but don't blow too hard or you get a face full of bran and mealworms. A blow dryer works also, set on low or cool.

2. Wash the mealworms. Use a strainer or colander with *very* small holes, and pat the mealworms dry.

3. ***This step requires parent supervision.** Spread the mealworms on a cooking tray—preferably one with sides so they don't crawl off. Roast in a 200-degree oven until dry and crunchy.

After that, I was on familiar ground blending butter and sugar and sprinkling chocolate chips.

I called my concoction Toffee Surprise, and chose to taste test it in a large group setting where peer pressure would encourage full participation. What better occasion than my mother's birthday! The verdict: The toffee was yummy and sweet with a subtle earthy aftertaste.

Since I got several thumbs up, I baked another batch and sent it to *Cricket* for my editor to try. I figured if I had to eat it so did he. Laurence Schorsch, then assistant editor, thanked me for the "surprisingly good" toffee, and added, "Most authors don't bother to send us edible vermin, so you'll be remembered around here for a long time."

Although I have never written another how-to since then (can you blame me?), I did learn a few important rules that go into writing a successful how-to article: Develop a kid-friendly topic, be aware of a child's abilities and safety issues, pay attention to details, and do it yourself so you can work out the bugs (no pun intended).

The How-to Format

The format of a hands-on, how-to magazine article follows an organized pattern much like a recipe.

1. Introduce the activity. In a magazine, the title might serve as your introduction. *Highlights*, for example, packs its craft page with up to six how-to's, so there is no lead paragraph. But often your opening paragraph will be the bait you dangle to entice a reader. Keep it short and sweet. Kate Hofmann, author of "Explore the World Beneath Your Feet," published in *Ranger Rick*, draws her readers in with these three sentences:

> Want to find out what's lurking in YOUR lawn? Explore the wild world under your feet with these make-at-home tools. This POOTER, or bug vacuum, will help you gently collect creatures for a closer look.

Right away she introduces what the project is: making a bug vacuum. And she uses language to her advantage, tapping into children's innate sense of wonder to motivate them into action. What budding entomologist could resist *exploring* the *wild creatures* lurking in their lawn?

2. Provide a materials list. Hofmann follows the format and, after her introduction, gives a list of materials that a child needs for the project. Written in a single column, it acts as a handy checklist for readers. Be thorough and specific. If the craft requires a clear plastic container, suggest what size, for example, a mayonnaise jar or a large soda bottle. Give suggestions as to where the items can be found. Hofmann's Pooter calls for 18 inches of aquarium tubing, which, she notes, can be found in most pet shops.

Children love to be able to gather up all the materials they need from the craft box, the recycling bin, or the pantry shelves and get to work when the mood strikes them.

It is helpful if the materials are easy to find, inexpensive, or free. Children love to be able to gather up all the materials they need from the craft box, the recycling bin, or the pantry shelves and get to work when the mood strikes them. Parents appreciate not having to drive out to the store for expensive materials, and editors welcome unusual and new ideas that involve the same old oatmeal boxes, plastic straws, and Pringles cans.

3. Give step-by-step directions. A numbered list is easier to follow than directions given in paragraph form, but no matter how you organize the instructions, clarity is key. Keep it simple.

Group instructions into a series of steps, but keep in mind that too many steps can be visually off-putting. One *Highlights* editor prefers no more than six steps, and *Pack-O-Fun* magazine often combines similar actions into a single step. For example, Step 2 in *Pack-O-Fun*'s instructions for making a Starry Night Lantern directs the reader to: "Remove lid from jar. Remove center of lid and screw outer rim back on jar. Position lights in jar with plug end at top."

Another example, from an article on making a Take a Hike Bottle Holder, combines the following instructions into a single step: "Measure and cut two 1 x 6 brown craft foam strips. Use pinking shears to trim one long side. Use black marker to write words like 'bike, camp, hike, run' on one strip." By combining a few directions into a single step it makes the process clear in the reader's mind. The next action—and the next step—moves on to a completely different set of tasks.

Always remember to inform the reader when an adult needs to be present. Projects that involve using the stovetop, oven, glue gun, or knife require parental supervision.

4. Write a brief conclusion. If you have a lead paragraph, you might want to conclude with a short section on how to use the item the child just made, or offer suggestions as to how the project can be adapted. Hofmann concludes her Pooter how-to with advice on how to improve your chances of catching a bug, while instructions in *Kiki* on how to design your own textile end with a few sentences on creating wallpaper or gift wrap.

Matching How-to Projects to Age Interests

When writing a how-to it's important to consider both the age and skill level of your reader. Some activities are more suited to particular age ranges, for example:

Youngest Readers—Very young children need simple steps and limited materials. Always recommend adult supervision and keep the task short, because young readers have limited attention spans. Examples: sticker projects, simple animal-related projects.

Intermediate Readers—Middle-grade readers have developed both the skills and patience to create. They love to make things and do experiments. This age group can follow a lengthy list of instructions (as long as they are clear) and stick with a task over time. Examples: food science experiments/data-gathering, inventions that solve problems.

Teen Readers—General how-to articles are slightly more common for teens than specific step-by-step procedures. Teens need room to inject their own sense of creativity and personality into a project. Examples: how to organize a walk-a-thon for charity, or make a movie using computer software.

The How-to Market

Instructional texts make up a large chunk of the nonfiction market. The practical benefits of how-to materials make them invaluable resources, and large numbers of people continue to be willing to pay for this type of information. If you have something new to offer, or a fresh take on a well-worn subject, this market is particularly welcoming. Whether you're working on a magazine article or a book, writing how-to also has practical and immediate benefits for the writer: It can help you begin to establish credibility in a specific field.

Writing How-to for Magazines

Magazine editors see numerous how-to submissions, but that doesn't mean your manuscript has to get lost in the shuffle. There are three tactics you can use to distinguish your article from the pack: 1) Write about perennial topics like holidays. 2) Target boys' interests. 3) Write for parents as well as children.

Write about Holidays

A majority of magazines cover major holidays like Christmas, Hanukkah, Halloween, and Valentine's Day, and the editors may be overwhelmed with submissions related to these holidays. So search out and target other kid-friendly celebrations that will catch an editor's attention. How about making a star chart to celebrate Galileo's birthday on February 15, or making a bird feeder to celebrate the Great Backyard Bird Count? Try International Pancake Day or National Teacher Day. Holidays celebrated in other countries open up new opportunities to teach about other cultures while also sharing a craft project. How about a project to go with the Chinese Lantern Festival, or Nag Panchami, the Indian festival of snakes? Check out websites like www.holidays.net or www.holidayinsights.com for inspiration.

> You will have a better chance of publication if you are one of the 10 percent of submissions that appeal to boys.

Target Boys' Interests

According to Kim Griswell, Senior Editor at *Highlights*, 90 percent of the how-to submissions the magazine receives have more "girl appeal." That means you will have a better chance of publication if you are one of the 10 percent of submissions that appeal to boys. On the whole, boys prefer active projects and crafts that can be played with or used after they are created, like paper airplanes, telescopes, bat houses, or homemade batteries. And they welcome anything messy, gross, or dirty. Sometimes boys need extra incentive to get involved, so try linking your craft to a school subject, Scouting badge, or other relevant interest.

Write for Children *and* Parents

If you have written a craft project for children, double the results of your research efforts by changing the slant and targeting that same craft to an adult market. Parenting magazines like *Family Fun* publish crafts to keep kids busy during the summer months or to celebrate special events. If your craft has a curriculum connection, target teacher's magazines. Make it clear how teachers could use the exercise in their classroom and what kinds of skills or lessons it will provide. Test your idea first. Contact your local school and ask if you could share your project with a class. It will benefit the students and help you get the kinks out of your instructions.

Writing How-to Books

If you have a collection of hands-on projects, you can gather them together to form the basis of a book. Many years ago I wrote a book with my friend Patricia Phibbs on how to make cornhusk crafts. Each activity featured a way to wrap, braid, bundle, twist, curl, coil, or weave cornhusks to create dolls, wreaths, mats, baskets, and flowers. We taught the basic skills in the first chapter to avoid repeating ourselves with each project.

The difference between a book and a magazine article is that, in a book, you can lead readers more deeply into the skill; the first project is typically the easiest with the more difficult ones at the end. Our first set of cornhusk instructions led readers through the process of making a basic traditional Indian doll. Later on, we demonstrated more complicated variations, like puffy-sleeved dresses and character dolls with movable joints.

Your materials don't have to be household items. When children choose to learn a new skill, their interest has already been piqued and they are ready for more information. They are more likely to purchase materials required for the project.

Some how-to books focus on a theme that unifies different types of hands-on activities. For example, Laurie Carlson's award-winning book, *Thomas Edison for Kids*, is primarily a biography with 21 activities that illustrate some aspect of Edison's inventions. Her other activity books, which also blend history, biography, and activities, include solid facts. The combination is a terrific way for kids to learn and have fun at the same time.

Author Carol Johmann goes out of her way to make sure her projects are based on fact. "I'm always looking for accuracy," she says, "but also to give the kids a real experience of how something was built." For her book, *The Lewis & Clark Expedition*, Johmann adapted the actual dimensions and sketches of the keelboat described in an expedition diary and scaled them down to the typical size of balsa wood.

Sometimes tracking the information is more difficult than the project itself. For the same book, Johmann wanted kids to make a Mandan Indian mud hut, but the only description of one she could find was a small paragraph in a colonel's journal. After a lengthy library search, she finally found a 1934 pamphlet that contained complete diagrams and schematics. Now she was assured that a child's construction would be an accurate representation scaled down to size.

> Accuracy can equal safety when writing about a sports topic like snowboarding or spelunking.

Accuracy can equal safety when writing about a sports topic like snowboarding or spelunking. Dana Rau, author of *Rock Climbing for Fun*, had personal experience climbing the White Mountains in New Hampshire and took a climbing class at the outdoor climbing tower of a local recreation center. But most importantly, she sat down with an experienced instructor to confirm her facts and capture the details she might have otherwise missed.

Themed how-to books that follow curriculum guidelines are highly sought after by librarians, teachers, parents, and kids. The ratio of factual information to activities can vary greatly, but the chief selling points are accurate information and fun projects that teach children about the world around them.

Sometimes a young person's quest for information relates less to making crafts and doing science experiments and more to overcoming problems and handling personal issues. Like how-to books, self-help books provide a set of guidelines or instructions for readers to follow as they learn a new skill or deal with a problem. The self-help market offers writers many publishing opportunities and a great sense of satisfaction as well.

Writing the Self-Help Manuscript

When we were researching the self-help market, Peggy checked out dozens of books and magazines from the library so we could examine the format and style. Flipping through a cartoony book called *HELP! A Girl's Guide to Divorce and Stepfamilies* by Nancy Holyoke, Peggy noticed that someone had taken the quiz and filled in her answers.

Q. When Mom picks you up at Dad's, the two of them get into a big fight. Afterward, Mom says, "What a jerk. Aren't you glad to be coming home?"

The question goes on to list three responses. The mystery girl circled answer *A: You say nothing.*

Q. One question has been gnawing at you all week: Are you going to have to move? Now here comes Mom to say good night.

The reader circled answer *C: You just smile and hug her. If you're very sweet and helpful, maybe she won't let the move happen.*

It broke Peggy's heart to think there was a young person in town—maybe someone she knew—suffering silently through her parents' divorce. Here was a *real* kid with *real* problems, and the advice given in that book had better be *real* good.

The success of a self-help book or article lies in its ability to offer trustworthy advice with an air of authority. You may be the authority figure if you are a teacher writing SAT study tips, but direct quotes from a dean of college admissions will give readers another level of advice, and show the editor that you went the extra mile to provide reliable information. Although Peggy and I have written more than 50 books between us, we consulted dozens of other writers and editors to give you the best possible advice on writing nonfiction, and to provide a variety of perspectives. If you are not an expert on the subject, that's okay, too. Your job as a writer is to bring the experts to your readers.

> The success of a self-help book or article lies in its ability to offer trustworthy advice with an air of authority.

Trudi Trueit, the author of several books in a Scholastic self-help series that tackles subjects such as divorce, ADHD, and eating disorders, relies on many experts for information. "I'm not a psychologist, so I talk to experts to find out what the perceptions are of what children are dealing with, and what the misperceptions are." She takes the information they give her and hones it down. "After they have explained something to me, I often say, 'Yeah, I can see that, but now talk to me like I'm twelve.'" This process helps her make the information understandable as well as accurate for her young readers. Trueit suggests that if you ever feel uneasy giving certain advice, don't. Let the experts say it for you.

But what happens when experts disagree? Trueit encountered conflicting advice while writing about ADHD, and presented both sides to the reader. No single treatment works for everyone, so by presenting several options she hoped to help more families find a viable solution.

The trick to writing self-help for kids is to avoid sounding preachy. One way to do this is to let young people speak for themselves. Illustrate the effectiveness of the advice with first-person anecdotes. In an article you may use only one or two real stories, but a book requires several. Finding kids who are willing to share their experiences can be challenging and makes the interview process more labor intensive, but the end result is worth it.

For each of her self-help books, Trueit asked specialists to assist her in locating families with children who would be willing to talk to her. Some therapists posted Trueit's request on their bulletin boards, while others encouraged their clients to participate as part of the healing process. It was always up to the families whether a teen gave an interview, and Trueit assured them they would remain anonymous. She even arranged for them to contact her through an online support group so they did not have to divulge their name, age, or address. Once she knew their stories, Trueit went back to the therapists, who suggested things the teens could do to help themselves. Incorporating quizzes to keep the material light, she effectively combined personal stories and trustworthy advice to create truly helpful books.

> Whether you're writing self-help or how-to, the reward remains the same: the knowledge that you've contributed something positive to the lives of your readers.

Trueit found it gratifying to connect with real teens. The way she sees it, "You are speaking out for them and you want to get the best information for them." Whether you're writing self-help or how-to, the reward remains the same: the knowledge that you've contributed something positive to the lives of your readers.

Chapter 10
Strengthening
Your True Story

- The Revision Process
- Line Editing
- Fact Checking
- Meeting Word Counts

Writing Conferences
and Critique Groups

"Experience has taught me that the best books are those that have been rethought, reconsidered, rewritten over and over again. I like to tell kids that I'm not a good writer, but I'm a great rewriter."
—Candace Fleming, author of *Amelia Lost*

It is truly a thrill to hold a completed first draft in your hands. You worked hard bringing your idea to fruition. The research may have taken weeks, months, or even years, and plotting and writing may have taken even longer. Take a deep breath and congratulate yourself. Filled with this sense of achievement it might be tempting to submit your first draft to an editor. But this is a temptation you should avoid. Submitting your manuscript too soon is like pulling a cake out of the oven before it is fully cooked. The cake may look done, but it is not ready to be served to company. Similarly, your manuscript is not ready for an audience until you have had a chance to revise.

Some novice writers have an aversion to revision as if it implies failure or wrongdoing. Those feelings may stem from the days when teachers returned every essay, book report, or poem graded and stained with red ink. But there are no grades here. Besides, at this point no one but you has even looked at the manuscript. It's a great place to be. You have a finished first draft and the opportunity to make it stronger before anyone else reads it. Seasoned writers know that the revision process is a necessity, but in some respects revising is a wonderful luxury, too. It is that do-over on the basketball court. A mulligan on the first tee. A free makeover before a class reunion. What a gift. So, remember, revision is not about fixing a failed manuscript; it's about solidifying your original vision. As you revise, new connections develop, ideas merge, and dead weight falls away.

It may help to rethink your concept of revision altogether. So often we see it defined as the final stage of the writing process, but its rightful place is hardly last. Think of an Olympian's training schedule. At the beginning of the season the athlete is fully capable of completing the course, but is in no way ready for a competitive race. But with each practice her reflexes quicken, muscles become more defined, and style is perfected until she is ready to compete on the world stage.

> Revision is not about fixing a failed manuscript; it's about solidifying your original vision.

The same is true for your manuscript. Your first draft is a weakling standing at the starting block. Each round of revision will strengthen and tone your prose, bringing it closer to publishable perfection. Award-winning author Katherine Paterson, who admittedly loves the revision process, put it beautifully when she said, "Where else in life can spilled milk be transformed into ice cream?" Conducting such a transformation requires guts. As editor and writer Jordan Rosenfeld says, "I think there is even greater reward in the revision process than the first draft gush, but it takes also a greater faith to get there. You have to believe in yourself, muster the courage to see what isn't working and not take it personally when it isn't." And watching your own manuscript turn into something special is well worth the effort.

The Revision Process

Don't be fooled by the heading of this section. There really is no single process that works for all authors. Some writers do revisions as they go, while others tend to get their initial thoughts down on paper and revise later. Most do a combination of both.

For Peggy and me, getting to the first draft has already taken much effort. We've rewritten sentences, hacked off paragraphs, stitched them back on, and severed them again. Our first draft is actually a culmination of many mini drafts. It is basically what we want, but it's flimsy and we are tired from the endeavor. That is why the first step in the revision process is Peggy's favorite part: Rest.

> Some writers do revisions as they go, while others tend to get their initial thoughts down on paper and revise later.

Before embarking on revisions, let your manuscript sit for a few days. Work on another story or, if you are like us and have left a few chores undone, vacuum the floors and mow the lawn. Don't rush it. "Those words," says Gail Martini-Peterson, "are so much a part of you that you'll probably skim over much that could be fixed." But step away from the project for a few days or a week, and you'll return to the manuscript with fresh eyes and a focused mind.

If you are on a deadline or don't have the time to let your manuscript rest, then try one of these tips to prevent what author Barbara Kerley calls reading on automatic pilot. "Since I compose at the computer, simply printing out the manuscript helps me see it in a new way," Kerley says. "Printing it out and taking the copy somewhere else—say, a coffee shop— helps, too. It's even different reading it sitting on the couch, instead of at my desk." Editor Stephen Roxburgh recommends printing the manuscript in triple-space or in a completely different font; anything that will wake up your brain so you see your words as if for the first time.

But what are you looking for? Or more importantly, what are you *listening* for? That's right. A key factor in effective revision is to read your manuscript aloud. C. S. Lewis once said, "Always write (and read) with the ear, not the eye. You should hear every sentence you write as if it was being read aloud or spoken." This simple technique will help you better identify places that need revision than just reading silently.

We have already gone through the essential elements of a successful nonfiction book or article. After you've applied them to your own story, it is time to revisit those elements and evaluate their effectiveness, starting with the big picture view.

Seeing the Big Picture

Read through your manuscript in its entirety. What is your initial impression of it now that you have a fresh perspective? Be honest, and consider the needs of your audience. Is the amount of information you've supplied appropriate for the age and knowledge level you have chosen to write for? Is it clear from the start what your focus is about? Is it tight enough for an article or does the information wander off topic?

> If you can easily pull a main point from each paragraph and plug all of them into a cohesive, logical outline, then you've done your job well.

I have found that now is the perfect time to create an outline, if I haven't already. Even outline-averse Peggy agrees. If you can easily pull a main point from each paragraph and plug all of them into a cohesive, logical outline, then you've done your job well. You will see clearly if the manuscript is balanced or if the pace drags, or if there are gaps in the information. Are all key points defined and illustrated with appropriate anecdotes or examples? Have you given minor points too much attention? You may need to cut long discussions that distract from your focus. If your primary focus should be the eating habits of an animal, for example, make sure the discussion of its name (scientific or otherwise) does not dominate the conversation.

Review your plotline. For instance, if you have employed a chronological framework, make sure that it is maintained throughout. Does the information progress from simple to complex or does it jump around? Ensure that your transitions lead your reader seamlessly from beginning to end.

Sizing Up Your Prose

Children's books and articles come in all shapes and sizes. The broad spectrum of children's ages accompanied by a wide-ranging set of reading skills and preferences requires precise targeting by authors, who should keep their audience in mind at all times during the writing process. The Big Picture review offers one more chance to double-check the appropriateness of your prose.

As a rule of thumb, a paragraph intended for the youngest readers should contain no more than two or three sentences or one basic concept. For middle-grade readers, you can add more in the way of illustration and example in a paragraph, and perhaps tie two concepts together, either in your topic sentence—creating a transition from the preceding paragraph—or within the paragraph itself. For teenagers, you can write much as you would for adults, but paragraphs should still be kept short, for visual appeal.

Most importantly, assess whether or not the manuscript is fresh and unique. Circle the new information that you have included or the innovative insights you are presenting. Remember that editors have seen thousands of manuscripts—will yours wake them up and make them take note? If you find that your manuscript rehashes information that other authors have already covered, consider digging a little deeper into your research or conducting an interview with a specialist in the field.

Zooming In

Once you have looked at the overall organization of your manuscript, now you can zoom in on storytelling and structural details. Review the elements of storytelling in Chapter 5 and consider whether you've used them effectively in your own writing.

- Have you set the scene? Are your details specific and clear? Will the reader be able to create a mental image?

- Underline the sensory detail that will put your reader in the proper time and place. If you haven't found any, consider where appropriate details could be added.

- Is there dialogue in the form of quotations? Are the quotes accurate and attributed to the correct person? Are they purposeful or do they repeat what you have already said? Here is an example of a common quotation revision:

> Shirley Chisholm enjoyed politics. She once said, "I thrive on the fight. That's why I love politics."

By deleting the lead sentence, you avoid the repetition and let the speaker's words take center stage:

> Shirley Chisholm said, "I thrive on the fight. That's why I love politics."

Next, review Chapter 6 to see if your story skeleton is assembled properly.

- Does your title attract readers' attention?

- Will your lead hook them or is it all "throat clearing?" Editor Barbara Lucas uses this term to describe leads that ramble until the *real* beginning appears on page three. She also calls these slow starts "feather dusting," because they are like the old-time theatrical productions that opened with the maid waving her feather duster over the furniture while she told the butler what the main characters were up to. Such tactics were used to set the stage, and let the audience know where the action would start when the curtain opened. But readers, especially young ones, don't sit still for feather dusting. They want to get into your true story right away.

- Is your ending logical and smooth rather than abrupt or jarring?

- Look at your headings and sidebars if you have them. They should all be formatted the same way.

Keeping Track of Revisions

Those of us who are old enough to remember carbon copies appreciate more fully the organizational benefits of computers for keeping track of progressive drafts. On my first book, if I wanted to make a change, I had to retype the entire section. Now I just cut and paste and save each session in case I change my mind and want to go back to the original rendition.

For each project, I create a file folder using the title for the folder name, such as ANATOMYOFNF. It sits right next to the ANATOMYOFNF_INTERVIEWS folder that is already bursting with documents such as "RandiRivers_Interview.doc." I save the first draft with a title like "AnatomyofNF_roughdraft.doc" or simply "AnatomyofNF1.doc." Each significant revision is saved in successive files.

Children's author Jan Fields uses an ingenious method to save drafts of magazine articles based on the market she is targeting. "Often I will do a revision for each possible magazine saved under different file names that include the magazine name, such as 'PlatypusLadybug.doc,' and then choose the version I like best when I make the final submission decision."

You may have a dozen versions of a manuscript on your computer before it is accepted by an editor; then you can create another folder for each round of editorial revisions.

Reading Line by Line

Line editing, or reading word by word, sharpens your prose even more. There are several valuable resources that you should use: a dictionary, a thesaurus, and a language and style book like *The Elements of Style* by Strunk and White. A careful line edit means that you should:

- Check spelling and punctuation. Peggy will be the first to admit that she is a terrible speller, and is thankful for the spell check tool on her computer. But she also knows that it won't catch misused homophones like *hear* and *here* or *effect* where it should read *affect*. Be your own spell checker.

- Listen for words that are repeated too frequently. Rephrase or look for a substitute word where necessary.

- Cross out commonly used phrases or clichés. Either state your case directly or create your own distinctive analogy.

- Look for sentences that could be active rather than passive. For example, "A loud cry could be heard," is a passive sentence because there is no subject performing the action. Change it to an active sentence by adding the subject: "The girl heard a loud cry."

- Check for repetitive sentence structures (similar subject/verb patterns) and add variety where possible, in structure and length.

Checking Fact by Fact

At this point, you should review your manuscript again for accuracy. This step is important because as you revise you might inadvertently alter the information. Make sure each sentence says what you want it to say.

- Double-check your facts.

- Review quotes for accuracy, and check attributions.

- Verify the spelling of proper names.

- If you have created a bibliography, check to see that all references have been included.

Meeting the Word Count

As your revision nears completion, check your word count. Are you on target? Meeting the word length requirement is especially important when writing an article. Editors will not do the cutting for you, so if your manuscript is over the limit it's up to you to make the necessary adjustments.

If only minor trimming is in order, look for passages where you may have given too many details or examples. Can you drop one without sacrificing the point you are trying to make? Delete unnecessary adjectives, adverbs, and other weedy words. Reshape rambling sentences so they are more concise. You'll be surprised at how many words you can eliminate this way.

Major cuts mean entire paragraphs will have to go. But first think about the core of your book or article. What is the single most important thing you want your reader to take away? Anything beyond that core is fair game for cutting. Also, look at the lead, which may be all "throat clearing." Can you start closer to the main point? Nudging the manuscript under the limit word by word is sometimes the only remaining remedy.

If your article is running short, the best course of action is to gather additional information through interviews. Whether you decide to talk again to someone you previously interviewed or speak to someone new, branch out your line of questioning to expand the manuscript's focus. You'll likely discover some interesting details about the topic that will add authenticity at the same time.

We know that the revision process can seem daunting. It is hard work; we won't deny that. But we promise that the process will grow easier over time because your writing will improve. Eventually, you will notice that you seldom use weedy words like *really* or *very*, and you no longer have to go back and add sensory detail because you wove it into the first draft. Soon you will see that rewriting has made you a better writer.

Writers Helping Writers: Getting a Second Opinion

After you have revised your manuscript—looking at the big picture first then zooming in on the details—you may be ready for a second opinion. The people you choose to read your manuscript should be able to give you constructive criticism. Your mother, husband, or wife will love it because they love you, and your friends may be amazed simply because they had no idea you wanted to be a writer. They may be *too* supportive. Writers need more than praise. We need an honest assessment.

Remember that Olympic athlete? She didn't train alone; she had coaches on the sidelines and fellow athletes huffing and puffing along the same track. The same is true for writers. There is plenty of help out there so that you do not have to revise alone. Enlist the aid of a writing partner or critique group, and go to writing classes and workshops to test whether your writing is truly fit to beat the competition.

> Writers need more than praise. We need an honest assessment.

Critique Groups

A writer's critique group is just what it sounds like—a group of writers who critically review each other's work. But choosing the group that's right for you is not like joining a social club. You have to find the right fit for your personality, your sensibilities, and your writing style and genre.

The first group I went to was made up of a news reporter, a couple of published poets, and magazine writers. Several people had not yet been published, and a few had not yet submitted any of their work. I was the only person writing for children. The rules were simple: You could read aloud one chapter of a book, a few poems, an article, or a short story.

Many members read their own work. Writers who wanted to hear their work asked another person to read it, which is a good way to identify unwanted repetition, awkward sentences, or boring bits.

Although this is a common critiquing format, it is not the only one. Other critique groups have first-page readings, intended to be representative of the portion that is typically read by the "first reader" at a publishing house. Publishers are deluged with thousands of manuscripts each month. The manuscripts that first readers pass on to an editor are almost always the ones with a great first page. If you ask editors what they look for, the answer is usually some version of "a fresh manuscript with an authentic voice." But if that isn't obvious from the first page the reader will most likely clip on a rejection slip and mark it for return.

> It's not unusual to try different critique groups before you find one that fits your needs or has the right comfort level.

Some writers prefer a written commentary or line-by-line editing directly on the page; they might join a critique group that exchanges manuscripts before the meeting. When they get together, each person returns the manuscript to its author with a written or oral critique. Drawbacks for the writer may include the amount of precious time it takes to read these critiques, and perhaps trying to incorporate everyone's ideas. And of course the drawback for the other members is time away from their own writing. But weighed against the help you give and receive, it could be time well spent, especially when you are starting out.

It's not unusual to try different critique groups before you find one that fits your needs or has the right comfort level. Peggy was once invited to an established critique group in a neighboring town. When she showed up, they made her feel welcome, but when members began to read their material it became clear that everyone's writing had a similar theme and a strong agenda that Peggy did not feel comfortable with. She sat through the meeting, but sent her apologies for not officially joining the group.

As a nonfiction writer, you might be the minority in a mostly fiction critique group. We asked many nonfiction writers if this was a concern, and they told us it was not a problem. In fact, it was an asset. Fred Bortz, a prolific nonfiction author who specializes in science topics, believes that by working with fiction writers, his nonfiction storytelling skills become stronger. Fiction writers are quick to hear where a nonfiction author veers off into telling facts rather than showing the true story. Listening to fiction and critiquing it also hones your storytelling skills.

Another nonfiction writer enjoys hearing what her fiction friends have to say. "I found them to be very helpful because they always nailed me if they couldn't follow my article." She is quick to note that the great thing about her critique group is that everyone writes for children—which may be key. Authors of adult material may not appreciate how difficult it is to achieve simplicity, brevity, or just the right gross factor. If you are lucky enough to be in a critique group that has other nonfiction writers, you'll also find it a great place to share research tips, contacts, and organizational ideas.

> Fiction writers are quick to hear where a nonfiction author veers off into telling facts rather than showing the true story.

When authors Richard and Janet Graber wrote their book, *I Couldn't Do It Without My Group: Secrets of Starting and Running a Successful Writers' Group*, they asked writers everywhere to describe their groups. They asked how many people were in the group, where they met, and how often, as well as what rules or guidelines they followed.

Although the Grabers conclude that there is no ideal group for everyone, their advice is: "If you are sincere about writing for kids and give it a top priority in your life, the give-and-take of a group can be instrumental in moving you along. Out of the group activity comes friendly trust that lets you reveal your writing (and yourself) to others and builds in you a sincere desire to seek and appreciate their honest reactions. You, in turn, help do the same for them."

The Ear of an Editor: Active Listening Skills for a Better Critique

The most important things to bring to a critique session are an open mind and a willingness to listen. But what do you listen for in a nonfiction manuscript? Color—descriptions that make you envision a scene. Crisp quotes that evoke some response—wonder, humor, or goose bumps. Listen for the nonfiction story line that starts with a great lead and follows through to a satisfying conclusion.

The Northern Ohio SCBWI website offers this list of questions to ask yourself as you listen to a nonfiction manuscript:

1. Does the introduction grab your attention? Does it make you want to hear more?
2. Do the facts flow in a logical sequence?
3. Do you understand? Does the author present enough facts and examples to make it clear?
4. Does the article have kid appeal? Is it interesting and lively?
5. Does the article keep your interest?
6. Does the writer show the facts or just tell about them by reciting information?
7. Is the writing targeted correctly for a particular age group? Is it too simplistic or too difficult?
8. Do you hear inconsistencies in the information or have unanswered questions?

As you listen, jot down your thoughts so you will remember to tell the author about them when it is your turn to comment. Don't rely on your memory. When you do express your opinion, first tell the writer what you liked, and give criticism with a positive spin by offering a suggestion on how a weak spot in the manuscript could be made stronger.

Critique Group Etiquette

Because the primary activity is critiquing someone's creative endeavors, it is important for everyone to be on their best behavior. A friend told us about a new member who jumped right in with such harsh criticism that another writer had to intervene and explain, "We usually try to say something nice first, and then offer suggestions for parts that need work." The next time it was the newbie's turn to react to a manuscript, he said, "Well, that's a nice blouse, but your story stinks." This anecdote spread and now we all get the message when someone in our group says, "Well, that's a nice blouse, but . . ."

To keep your critique group running smoothly everyone should follow the same guidelines. Be positive. Offer your criticism with helpful advice. For example, if you nearly nodded off during the reading because the manuscript dragged, you could suggest that the writer add more dialogue to quicken the pace.

H. G. Wells once wrote, "No passion in the world is equal to the passion to alter someone else's draft." But don't get carried away. The most helpful comments are your reactions to scenes, action, and accuracy. Can you see the setting? Did you feel anything? Is the argument understandable? Offer your honest opinion and helpful suggestions. For example: "I liked your description of the Spanish warship, but I didn't understand what you meant in that first paragraph."

Being Critiqued

New writers can be devastated by a first critique. So there are rules for them, too. Remember that your critique group is there to help you. We have met people who don't want to read their work because they're afraid someone might steal their idea. Believe it or not, that's unlikely to happen. Even if you are writing about a similar subject, or have a similar plot, no two writers have the same voice or the same view of the material. So relax, be open to someone else's opinion, and mind the following:

- **Bring your best work.** Get the most out of a critique by bringing your finest effort. Do not bring a hastily written first draft. Give yourself time to edit and revise your manuscript to the best of your ability before inviting comment from others.

- **Listen to someone else read your manuscript out loud.** It gives you the advantage of hearing the cadence of your sentences, or noticing a jarring phrase that doesn't quite convey what you meant or a paragraph that can be tightened or expanded.

- **Pay attention when it's time for others to critique your manuscript.** Be open-minded. Take notes, and ask questions if you don't understand the suggestions or comments.

- **Consider each comment carefully.** Whatever is suggested in a critique group is just that—a suggestion, an opinion. In the first group I attended, one member took careful notes of everyone's comments about her manuscript. The following week, she returned with the same article, but she had added and changed lines to include every suggestion. It was no longer her article. There was little left of her style or voice or opinions. Her manuscript had turned into a camel, a horse created by committee. In defense, she said, "But you told me to change that." Think about the comments and use or discard what you will. Do someone's remarks ring true or spark an idea that will improve your story? If more than two people make the same suggestion, it is a strong sign that a problem exists.

- **Avoid arguing.** It only hampers the process. Take in each comment with an open mind. It's better to be aware of possible problems before you send the manuscript to an editor.

- **Don't monopolize the time.** Avoid asking endless questions to get more advice. Listen to what is said and move on to the next person's manuscript. Good critiques, like good ideas, need time to incubate. At first a comment might not make sense, but days or weeks later, you might have an "aha!" moment when a group member's remark comes back to you just in time to fix a section you are struggling with.

When you enter a group that doesn't feel comfortable or quite right for you for any reason, it's perfectly all right to make a change. There are many valid reasons: Are you the only children's writer? Is criticism too harsh or too superficial? Is there one person who wastes time, dominates the conversation, or brings up irrelevant topics? Does the meeting time meet your needs? If you have young children, or if you work all day, you may prefer an evening meeting. If you're retired or if you work from home, a daytime meeting may be better. Or maybe the only good time for you is at 2 A.M. while you are sitting in your pajamas. In that case an online critique group might be just right for you.

Critiquing Online

Neither one of us has ever participated in an Internet critique group, so we asked around. Everyone we talked to feels that online groups are useful, practical, and just as rewarding as face-to-face meetings, or more so. One online critique fan said, "I never knew how helpful or thoughtful other people could be regarding helping me with my writing. I wouldn't be where I am today without my group!" Mary Meinking Chambers, a frequent contributor to children's magazines and a member of four online critique groups, appreciates the peer pressure they exert. "A critique group gives me a push to create something new. It'd be much easier to procrastinate and put off writing when life gets busy. But a critique group forces me to write . . . which is good." And Cathy Nanz says, "It's a great alternative for people who simply can't commit to a personal meeting with someone, but who might be able to critique at odd hours."

To find an already established online group or to set up a new one, look on established websites like the Society of Children's Book Writers and Illustrators (SCBWI) website (www.scbwi.org), Children's Writers Retreat (http://Institutechildrenslit.net), or Verla Kay's Message Board for Children's Writers & Illustrators (www.verlakay.com). Be specific about your needs. Are you a beginner who hasn't submitted yet, submitting but not published, or a published author? Are you looking for a nonfiction-only critique group? Are you willing to use private emails to receive manuscripts or would you prefer to use a private list set up on a website like Yahoo? There are mixed-media groups that include novelists, picture book authors, and nonfiction writers all together and there are special-ized groups for just one genre. Most writers we spoke to feel that online critiques work well when the groups are homogenous. Critiques are less effective when some members are writing picture books, others are working on novels, and some are crafting nonfiction. "It's a bit like cri-tiquing a science paper when you flunked science," says Nanz. "If you don't know the format basics, etc. you can't really provide a thorough critique."

Online critique groups abide by the same rules as traditional groups: Submit only your best work; leave your ego in the desk drawer; try to meet the deadlines; and be posi-tive and supportive. Gail Martini-Peterson, author of the article "Critiquing in Your Jammies" at

> Soon your online critique group will become like far-flung members of your family.

www.InstituteChildrensLit.com, acknowledges that the process might take some getting used to. "Without facial expressions, online can be colder than face-to-face."

Manuscripts are typically sent via email, and comments and line-by-line edits are made in CAPS or in a different color so they stand out from the rest of the text. It may take several sessions to feel comfortable with the process and learn to distinguish helpful comments from the not-so-helpful ones. But soon your online critique group will become like far-flung members of your family, and you'll have added incentive to trav-el to out-of-town writer's conferences so you can finally meet in person.

Starting a Critique Group

If there are no established writer's groups in your area, and online critiquing is not for you, start your own critique group. To find members, post notices at local libraries, bookstores, and on reliable writers' discussion boards like the SCBWI critique group discussion board. Talk it up. Tell everyone you know. You may be pleasantly surprised to find children's writers lurking unnoticed in your hometown.

Before you start, there are several things to consider. What kind of writers do you want to attract? A group made up solely of novice writers may not know how to critique effectively, and may turn into just a cheering section. They may keep your spirits up but won't make you a better writer. A mix of novice writers and experienced or published authors works well. The experienced members can provide more insightful comments as well as much needed marketing information.

Where will your group meet? The number of members is often determined by the size of the meeting place, especially if you meet in members' homes. Bookstores, libraries, or other public places might allow you to expand the group or give more latitude for time and space, but may not be as intimate or consistent.

How often will you meet—weekly, every other week, or once a month? Meeting too often may be stressful if you have another job or if you are not used to producing new material every seven days. Our small group tried to meet once a month, but because we live an hour from each other, we can't always stick to the schedule, especially during Western New York winters. When we do meet, we bring a bag lunch, a snack to share, and a manuscript. Writing can be a lonely profession, so it's fun to spend a day with other writers who celebrate your successes, give you ideas, and provide comfort when you get a rejection. And we laugh a lot!

SCBWI

The Society of Children's Book Writers and Illustrators (SCBWI) is the only international organization devoted to the art of children's literature. It has more than 19,000 members worldwide and holds two major conferences each year: in New York City in the winter, and in Los Angeles in summer. It also sponsors meetings, workshops, and conferences in every state, as well as abroad. Members receive its newsletter, which offers up-to-date information on just about everything going on in the children's book business, including editorial staff changes, publishers' submission policies and needs, new publications and awards, and helpful how-to articles. Check out its website at www.scbwi.org.

Conferences and Workshops

Judging by the number of conferences and workshops listed in the SCBWI *Bulletin*, you could do nothing for a year but go from one conference to another across the country and back, and then on to workshops overseas. A conference typically provides the opportunity to network and learn the business. There are often several speakers, including a keynote speaker and others who lead smaller group sessions. Workshops are more hands-on than conferences. For example, you may spend each morning in critique or writing sessions getting to know one instructor well, then spend the afternoon listening to guest speakers or other workshop leaders.

Both workshops and conferences are held just about anywhere—on cruise ships, in church basements, at resort hotels, on college campuses, in libraries, at Holiday Inns, and in bookstores. But no matter what the venue looks like, conferences are a great way to expand your writing circle and gain much needed insight into the children's publishing business.

With so many events out there, it can be hard to choose the best one for you. One consideration is cost. A weekend conference is typically less expensive than a workshop that spans the entire week, but ask if there are single-day options that may help cut expenses and still give you a taste of the experience. Local conferences or workshops will also save you the expense of room and board at a conference out of state. You can save additional money by carpooling with members of your critique group or other writers in your area.

Another consideration is your level of experience and what you need. Are you a beginner learning the basics like manuscript format, word counts, and storytelling techniques, or are you already published and seeking information on promotion, contracts, and getting an agent? Most conferences try to provide a wide range of information to attract a large number of participants, so look at the workshop titles to make sure you will get the most out of the experience.

Who are the speakers? As nonfiction writers, we like to see at least one presenter on the schedule who has written nonfiction and will be addressing some aspect of it. Writer's workshops or retreats may be more genre-specific. In the past the Highlights Foundation has offered work-shops on nature writing as well as biography. If editors or agents will be at a conference, find out if they publish nonfiction or represent nonfiction writers.

With so many publishing houses closing their doors to unsolicited manuscripts, conferences are one of the few ways to make contact. As a courtesy, an editor who is speaking at a conference will usually look at manuscripts from writers who are in attendance for a certain period of time. Conference organizers give editors a list of names to look for so they are not inundated with submissions from people who were not at the conference.

More and more conferences are offering manuscript critiques for an additional fee. Take advantage of these offers. It is well worth the money

The Writer's Bookshelf: On Revision and Motivation

Bird by Bird: Some Instructions on Writing and Life by Anne Lamott, Anchor, 1995.

I'd Rather Be Writing by Marcia Golub, Writer's Digest Books, 2001.

Reading Like a Writer: A Guide for People Who Love Books and For Those Who Want to Write Them by Francine Prose, Harper Perennial, 2007.

Word Magic for Writers by Cindy Rogers, Writer's Institute Publications, 2004.

Writing It Right! How Successful Children's Authors Revise and Sell Their Stories by Sandy Asher, Writer's Institute Publications, 2009.

to have a professional writer, or better yet, an editor, read your manuscript. There is no guarantee that the keynote speaker or an editor will read it, but the caliber of the critique will still be high because the 20 or 30 manuscripts are divided among the guest speakers and published writers who have organized the conference. You'll get sound advice and make a valuable connection in the writing business.

Without fail, at every conference and workshop, a writer asks an editor or agent, "What are you looking for?" Most editors can tell you only that their company is looking for good middle-grade fiction, for example, or that they are swamped with picture books, so don't send those right now, or they only publish nonfiction. (Make note of that one!) No editor is likely to be more specific, because books are like a teacher's description of a perfect student. "No two are alike."

The best advice when talking to editors is to be yourself. Get to know them as people first and let them get to know you. Chances are they will remember the woman with six kids and a passion for horse stories more fondly than someone who shoved a manuscript under their nose during dessert.

Does meeting an editor at a conference ever pay off? Jo S. Kittinger, a regional advisor for the Southern Breeze chapter of SCBWI, says yes. She has hosted several conferences where editors have ended up signing writers who had attended their talks. "So," says Kittinger, "sometimes things happen just because you are in the right place at the right time, networking with people in the industry."

> The best advice when talking to editors is to be yourself.

The best part of a conference is meeting people who love to write. Published writers and those who haven't finished a manuscript yet will become your new friends and friendly competitors. They know what it's like to write on a lunch break or after everyone's in bed for the night. You'll be amazed at how willing writers are to share what they have learned, recommend a research source, or offer a warning against an unscrupulous agent. When you are ready to submit your manuscript, they may even suggest the perfect market.

Chapter 11
Flexing Your
Marketing Muscles

r-- Cover/Query Letters

Proposals

Contracts -----

The Publishing Process

"I believe that a book that knows why it is being written, for whom, and most important, what it wants to say, is a book well on its way to successful publication."

—Susan Rabiner and Alfred Fortunato, authors of *Thinking Like Your Editor*

I magine that you are an editor staring at a pile of manuscripts on your desk. One submission is wrapped in rainbow gift paper and sealed with sparkly stars. It looks intriguing, but you've been an editor long enough to know that this package is from a writer who has never been published. Like many other editors, you have seen everything: a manuscript delivered in a pizza box, another stuffed in a shoe, and a book proposal accompanied by a box of freshly baked brownies. You shared the brownies with your staff, and heaven knows what was done with the shoe, but the manuscripts were returned.

These are common stories. One editor we know received a square box with no return address or letter inside. "The box contained a stuffed toucan—that's it!" she says. She thought it was some kind of marketing ploy, so she put it aside, wondering what it was all about. Two weeks later, she received a manuscript that had a toucan as the main character. "Needless to say, the manuscript and the toucan flew the coop!"

This editor adds a few other comments. "I find that I can't go to a party without someone approaching me with, 'You work at a publishing house?' When I (reluctantly) say yes, they (or their friend or relative) inevitably have a manuscript that I would surely be interested in. I've even been cornered in the ladies room by prospective submitters! Another slush [pile] nightmare is when people send material that is wildly inappropriate for our publishing house," she says. "For example, we publish children's books, but someone sent us a manuscript about their personal genealogy."

> Submitting a manuscript is similar to applying for a job.

Writing for children is a business, and in order to get your manuscript into the hands of editors you have to understand that business and your role in it. Learn the submission process, develop the essential tools you'll need to flex your marketing muscle and target the appropriate publications, and you will become part of the publishing process.

Tools of Submission

Submitting a manuscript is similar to applying for a job. You wouldn't go to an interview wearing old jeans and dirty sneakers, with no credentials in hand. You'd stick to the timeworn cliché to put your best foot forward. Do that for your nonfiction too.

Start with a double-spaced manuscript neatly typed in an easy-to-read font such as Times Roman or Courier. Give your editor ample margins to write in, an inch will do. And provide your name and address in the upper left corner of the first page, as well as your name on each following page, to help identify a loose sheet should the wind snatch the editor's briefcase while he is waiting for the A-train.

The additional tools for submitting a manuscript are the same whether you are writing a nonfiction article or a book manuscript. You'll need a professional, intriguing cover letter, query letter, proposal, and resume, and access to current market guides and publishers' guidelines.

Market Guides and Publishers' Guidelines

The best investment you can make is to purchase one or more market guides such as *Magazine Markets for Children's Writers*, *Book Markets for Children's Writers*, or *Writer's Market*. These publications compile information from hundreds of publishers in one handy book and are updated each year. As you flip through one, notice that every listing describes exactly what that publisher's editors are looking for—fiction genres, specific kinds of nonfiction, articles between 500 and 1,000 words, a complete manuscript, or just queries. For example, a recent edition of *Magazine Markets for Children's Writers* described *Faces* magazine's submission policy as: "Query with outline, bibliography, and clips or writing samples. Accepts email queries to facesmag@yahoo.com. Responds in 5 months."

Many market guides also provide additional insight from editors regarding submissions. In the same magazine guide, the editors of *JAKES Magazine* comment, "We like our feature stories to be supplemented by sidebars, bulleted lists, subheads, and other kid-friendly graphic elements."

Don't have a current market guide? Most magazine and book publishers also post their submission guidelines online. If a publisher has taken the time to explain its submission policy, then take these words to heart. Do not be the writer who sends a picture book to a company that does not publish picture books, in the hope that yours will be the one to change that policy.

After reading in the market guides that editors may take up to a year to respond to your submission it is tempting to save time by sending your manuscript to several publishers at once. But a nonfiction manuscript is not like a generic resume to employers who are looking for a general hire. Your manuscript, proposal, or query should be crafted to a particular publisher's needs. Learn about that publisher's preferences and how your manuscript will fit into its list. Think of it this way: Editors are acquiring more than a product or a part-time employee. They are discovering a new talent who they hope will write more for them. That's well worth your patience.

Cover Letters

Whenever you send a complete manuscript always add a cover letter. It is placed on top of the manuscript, or "covers" it. The editor will read this letter first, so it acts as a brief introduction to you and your work.

> Editors are acquiring more than a product or a part-time employee. They are discovering a new talent who they hope will write more for them.

Editors' desks are swamped in proposals, manuscripts, and contracts. They don't have time to read a chatty cover letter that lists your alma mater or details about the time you read your manuscript to your daughter's fourth-grade class. Keep your cover letter short and to the point. A basic letter includes: the title and word count of your manuscript, a brief description of the topic, and any previous publishing experience. If you have not been published before, then do not mention it. Other pertinent information might include:

- How your article fits with a publisher's theme.

- Why you are uniquely qualified to write this particular book or article. For instance, are you an expert in the field, or do you have personal experience related to the subject?

- How is your work different from other books or articles on the same topic? Will you include new research, or do you have a unique approach to the subject? Or maybe your story features first-hand accounts or interviews with people in the field.

- Always mention if you have made previous contact with the editor at a conference. For example: "I enjoyed meeting you at the SCBWI conference in Dallas last year. Your workshop on contemporary biographies inspired me to submit this manuscript about Kim Phuc, a child victim of the Vietnam War and founder of the Kim Foundation International. I hope you enjoy it."

Businesslike doesn't always mean impersonal. As an editorial assistant at Harcourt, Gretchen Hirsch appreciated a cover letter that was warm and natural. "The ones I like best are the ones that try to make a connection." Mention books the editor has worked on or a speech he or she gave that you liked, and then pitch your story.

Sample Cover

This cover letter accompanied a manuscript that Peggy sold to *Cricket* magazine. Notice that she briefly introduces the subject, mentions that it is a different slant on a common subject, and outlines her research. She concludes with a short list of some of her writing credits.

Dear Ms. Messina:

Every child knows that George Washington was our first president, but they'd be fascinated to learn that his first love was farming. I have enclosed a 1,100-word nonfiction article called "Farmer Washington Plants a Nation" that highlights the earthier side of Washington's life.

My research focused on Washington's own words and his personal diaries and correspondence, as well as noted biographies and information provided by the staff at Mount Vernon.

I am the author of nine nonfiction books for children and young adults including *Forensic Anthropology* for Facts on File, and *Reptile Rescue* and *Bird Alert* for Millbrook Press.

I hope you enjoy "Farmer Washington," and I look forward to hearing from you.

Sincerely,
Peggy Thomas

Query Letters

Many publishing houses and magazine editors require you to query before sending a manuscript. A query letter simply asks an editor if he or she would like to see your story. Cheryl Klein, senior editor at the Scholastic imprint Arthur A. Levine, likens the query letter to a pick-up line in the dating process. A good one will show off your stellar personality, demonstrate that you are well spoken, and, of course, look sharp (no typos).

In a short space, you need to provide the flavor of the manuscript and entice the editor with bits of story.

Charlesbridge, like many publishers that require query letters, has one exception. "A query letter is not necessary for a picture book for us," says Editor Randi Rivers, "because the [manuscript] is so short that it takes less time for an editor to read the story than to read and respond to the query. But a short chapter book, middle-grade book, or young adult book benefits from a brief query letter." *Brief* is the key word.

A well-crafted query should contain basic information such as the title of your manuscript and the subject matter, but it also needs to attract the editor's attention just as your well-written manuscript would. In a short space, you need to provide the flavor of the manuscript and entice the editor with bits of story. When asked what she looks for in a good query letter, Rivers says, "For me personally it's the tone of the piece, a different way of telling the story. I'm looking for strong writing skills . . . and engaging writing. It might be a subject I've seen before, but if it is told in a different way, that catches my eye."

Sample Query Letter

Here is a sample query letter that Peggy sent to Carolyn Yoder at Calkins Creek. Peggy had already worked with Yoder on another project, so the letter begins and ends informally.

Dear Carolyn:

Some kids called Roger "Professor Nuts Peterson." He'd carry a snake in his pocket or a bird's egg in his cap. He looked as thin and gawky as a fledgling egret and sometimes smelled of skunk. But this unruly, self-taught naturalist grew to become the leader of the conservation movement, a renowned artist, and the best-selling author of the revolutionary Peterson Field Guides that made bird watching a household hobby.

For the Birds is a 2,877-word picture book manuscript that tracks Roger Tory Peterson from his childhood in Jamestown, New York, to an art student in New York City, to world-famous naturalist. Although there are children's versions of Peterson's Field Guides, there are no children's biographies that highlight this fascinating man's struggles and perseverance to pursue what he loved most—birds.

The majority of my research took place at the Roger Tory Peterson Institute in Jamestown, where the bulk of Peterson's personal papers are archived. I had access to his childhood birding journals, his letters to friends and family, early sketches, and all of Peterson's published works.

If you would like to see the full manuscript, I would be happy to send it to you.

Take care,
Peggy

Peggy's query in the sidebar on page 207 loosely follows the format used by Pat Cronin Marcello, a veteran magazine writer, who recommends a four-part approach to query writing. The first paragraph is the *hook*, which frequently doubles as the lead in the article or book itself. In this case, the first three sentences of the query letter are also the beginning lines of Peggy's manuscript. An exciting anecdote, oh wow! facts, or a well-phrased question will also pique the editor's attention.

The second paragraph tells the editor what the manuscript is about. It is a 2,877-word picture book manuscript. Klein cautions about emphasizing word counts and other numbers. "It is equivalent to taking your date out and reciting your ACT or IQ scores. Interesting, but only relevant if the rest of it works out." Other editors, however, appreciate not having to search for that detail later on. Peggy also adds the fact that there are no similar biographies currently on the market; there is no competition.

The third paragraph should be all about you and why you are the best person to write this story. In Peggy's query, she highlights her research and the use of primary sources. This paragraph should also include the author's publishing experience, but because Yoder was already familiar with her background, Peggy left it out. If you have published before, mention your most recent credits. If you are hoping that this is your first sale, don't mention it. Let strong writing speak for itself.

The last paragraph sums up your project and can add spice to the pot with additional information. Are photos or other artwork available? When can you send the complete proposal or manuscript for their consideration? Say thank you and indicate the enclosure of a self-addressed stamped envelope (SASE), unless the guidelines say otherwise.

Many market guide listings recommend sending writing samples along with a query letter. If you have been published before, send along a photocopy of an article or chapter from a previous work, preferably similar to the age level and style of the piece you are proposing. If you have not been published, include a couple of pages from your manuscript to show your style and voice.

The Writer's Bookshelf: Selected Titles for Marketing and the Business of Children's Publishing

Author Law A–Z: A Desktop Guide to Writers' Rights and Responsibilities by Sallie Randolph, Capital Books, 2005.

Book Markets for Children's Writers, Writer's Institute Publications (annual editions).

Children's Writer's & Illustrator's Market, Writer's Digest Books (annual editions).

The Complete Idiot's Guide to Publishing Children's Books, 3rd edition, by Harold Underdown, Alpha Books, 2008.

The Giblin Guide to Writing Children's Books, 4th edition, by James Cross Giblin, Writer's Institute Publications, 2006.

It's a Bunny-Eat-Bunny World by Olga Litowinsky, Walker & Co., 2001.

Magazine Markets for Children's Writers, Writer's Institute Publications (annual editions).

Negotiating A Book Contract: A Guide for Authors, Agents and Lawyers by Mark L. Levine, Asphodel Press, 2009.

Thinking Like Your Editor by Susan Rabiner and Alfred Fortunato, W. W. Norton & Company, 2002.

Writer's Guide, Writer's Institute Publications (annual editions).

The Writer's Guide to Queries, Pitches & Proposals, 2nd edition, by Moira Allen, Allsworth Press, 2010.

A Writer's Resume

Some editors, especially those who work in the educational market, may request a resume. They don't want to know what your summer job was in college, but what your writing credits include. When an editor reads your resume, she is looking for three things: Can you write? Can you work with an editor? And what specialty, if any, do you have?

If you have a large inventory of writing credits lead with that. List your credits starting with the most recent. Organize them into categories: children's nonfiction books, magazine articles, professional or business writing, etc. Note the publisher and publication date, and any awards or honors you have received. If you do not have many writing credits but have experience in teaching, put that at the top of your page under a heading such as TEACHING EXPERIENCE. List the positions you have held and any curriculum work you have done. Teaching skills will be especially attractive to publishers who produce curriculum-related products. Also include your academic background. What degrees do you hold and what fields did you study?

At the bottom of the page, note your personal interests if they pertain to the topic you are presenting, particularly if you have pursued them with passion. Letting an editor know that you are a stamp collector may make you just the right person to write a beginner's guide to philately.

Editors usually keep a nonfiction writer's resume on file for a year or more. Don't think you are lingering in obscurity. We have been assured that these files do get looked at. When a book editor starts a new series, she will flip through the resumes looking for writers who are perfect for the project.

Book Proposals

A proposal is a package of information that aims to sell your idea; it is typically used to market a middle-grade or young adult book manuscript. It may include an expanded cover letter, a brief outline or table of contents, a sample chapter or two, and other supporting material.

Before you can write a proposal, you have to do enough subject research to know that the project is feasible, and market research to find out which publisher, if any, would be interested. You have to know what you want to write about, what you want to say about that topic, and how you want to say it. A savvy editor will read between the lines. According to Rabiner and Fortunato, an editor can read a proposal and tell if a writer demonstrates a command of the material, writes well, knows how to pull a reader into her nonfiction world, and above all, has passion for her subject.

In your expanded cover letter, highlight your best selling point. It might be the topic itself. Is it a subject that hasn't been written about before? Have you uncovered new information about an old issue? Or the timing of the manuscript might be important. A biography on Victoria Woodhull, the first woman to run for president, would tie in nicely with a presidential election year. Or perhaps your experience or expertise will be the key ingredient to getting that contract. Whatever it is, your selling point will be your primary sales pitch. In your expanded cover letter, describe your book and how it is distinctive from other books published on this topic.

> An editor can read a proposal and tell if a writer demonstrates a command of the material, writes well, knows how to pull a reader into her nonfiction world, and above all, has passion for her subject.

Let the editor know that you have researched the market. Are other books on the subject out of date or for a different age level than your proposed title? Perhaps your idea of using historic photographs would set the proposed book apart from other titles that are illustrated.

Give a brief description of your expertise, or a list of credits. Keep it professional. If you are an optometrist and are writing about eye care, let the editor know. Rivers adds, "It is nice to see people mention in proposals or cover letters that they've run the piece by an expert or they've included a great bibliography. In both of these cases, the writer has gotten across that they know what they are talking about."

The second part of your proposal is a chapter-by-chapter outline. Keep it brief and exciting. It shows how you will organize the material as well as what each chapter will contain. Start with a chapter title and follow that with a paragraph or two of the contents. Focus on the most exciting key points but don't get bogged down in detail. Each chapter should logically follow the previous one.

Sample Chapter Outline

We can hardly believe it ourselves, but this is a portion of the outline we sent to the editor at Writer's Institute Publications as part of the proposal for this book. You'll notice it gives the flavor of our style and a hint of what would go in each chapter. You'll also note that, in the end, we did not adhere strictly to these chapter outlines. Talks with our editor and information we uncovered during research added to the final result.

Outline for
TELLING TRUE STORIES: The Anatomy of Nonfiction
By Margery Facklam and Peggy Thomas

INTRODUCTION

This book is the collaboration of two nonfiction authors who happen to be mother and daughter. It is the sum of what we have learned in the process of researching and writing many magazine articles and more than 50 books of nonfiction. We have examined the anatomy of nonfiction to show you how to assemble these parts into your own body of work. In researching the art of nonfiction, we found that its many facets were as difficult to describe as the parts and processes of the human body, a task both of us have had to tackle. So we looked for second, third, and fourth opinions, and consulted specialists.

CHAPTER ONE: THE ANATOMY OF NONFICTION

Fiction is fun because anything can happen. But nonfiction authors have to stick to facts. Nonfiction sounds like a nonentity, when it is just the opposite. It is everything that is real. It is every true story, from the life of a single atom to a giant sequoia. It is our past and our present; every person who ever lived, every word spoken, every game played, every bridge built, and every inventive thought. You will never run out of true stories to tell.

This chapter will discuss nonfiction writers' view of their art, and how they came to write true stories. We'll explore different kinds of nonfiction, and take the pulse of nonfiction in the market today.

An example of a sidebar for this chapter: Honors and awards given for children's nonfiction.

CHAPTER TWO: BRAINSTORMING

The old adage, "Write what you know" is a good place to start. But it's too limiting. If we had confined ourselves to what we knew when each of us began to write, we might very well have written about PTA meetings and pediatricians.

This chapter will help you find the kinds of ideas that will fascinate readers and also hold your attention through the months of research, writing, and rewriting. Do you have enough information for a book-length manuscript, or is your topic better suited to a magazine? Often you can use the information for both. Once you've settled on a subject, how can you write it in a way that will compete with other books already on the market? And how do you decide what age group to write for?

An example of a sidebar for this chapter: The Frankenstein Factor—writing more than one article from your research.

CHAPTER THREE: UNCOVERING THE BONES

An archaeologist digs through tons of soil to sift out tiny bone fragments that will tell the story of a past life. A nonfiction writer must sift through thousands of bits of information for just the right facts that will tell the true story.

This chapter will describe where and how to find information in books, journals, and online. And you will surely want to talk to experts in the field. But how do you find an expert, and how do you prepare for the interview? What is a primary source and where can you find it?

An example of a sidebar for this chapter: Six things to do before a phone interview.

Next in your proposal package you'll put a polished first chapter. This is your chance to shine, so take your time crafting it. One common question is: Should I always enclose the first chapter, or can it be one that is more exciting? We feel that if your first chapter is not as exciting as the rest, you may need to reorganize or revise.

Some editors may need an extra bit of ammo when they are at the editorial table fighting for your book. What is the market potential of your manuscript? When Peggy pitched her picture book, *Joshua the Giant Frog*, she let editor Nina Kooij at Pelican Publishing know that it was a retelling of a folktale that originated along the banks of the Erie Canal in the 1800s, a topic that is part of the New York State school curriculum. As a result, the book could be easily integrated into social studies and language arts programs throughout the entire state.

This kind of market analysis, as it is called, may sound overwhelming, but chances are you have already done it. You went to the library to scope out the competition before deciding that your book was sufficiently different to warrant your time and talent. If you haven't, then get there now. Sneed Collard III, author of more than 20 nonfiction books, says that his market analysis involves searching for similar titles by age level on Amazon.com, and noting the publication dates. (The advantage to this method is that he also gets advance notice on forthcoming books.) Books that are older than three or four years need not be considered competition unless they are award-winners.

> In a sentence or two, you'll let the editor know how marketable your project will be and that you are serious about the business.

In your proposal you should be able to confidently say, "There are no current kayaking books for this age level." Or assure the editor that, "There has not been a new book on this subject since 1995, and with the recent discovery, it is time for an update." In a sentence or two, you'll let the editor know how marketable your project will be and that you are serious about the business.

Making A Sale

Although many writers claim that they would write regardless of a pay-check, it is nice to get paid for your work, especially if you intend to make writing your career as many nonfiction writers do. When you are starting out, it is perfectly acceptable to submit your work to magazines that may only offer three contributor's copies, because those articles will be the clips that you can send to other editors with larger budgets. But have enough confidence in your work to know when it is time to make that first real sale. And in the meantime, learn about the financial side of writing. What will they pay you? When will you be paid? And what exactly are you selling?

Selling a Magazine Article

Magazine publishers pay their writers in a variety of ways. Some offer a flat fee for a certain type or length of article. For example, *The Family Digest* pays $40–$60 for articles ranging from 700 to 1,200 words, and $24 for anecdotes. Other publishers pay by the word, anywhere from five cents to one dollar. *BYU Magazine* pays $.50 per word and accepts articles from 1,000 to 3,000 words. If you sold a 2,000-word article to *BYU* you would earn $1,000.

> Electronic rights should be negotiated separately than first rights or other rights; if they aren't spelled out clearly in the contract, then ask.

But what does the publisher get for that $1,000? *BYU* states that it purchases first North American serial rights, which means it buys the right to be the first to print your article in Canadian and U.S. markets. After that, rights revert back to you, and you are free to sell the article as a reprint to another magazine.

Publishers may also ask for electronic rights, which allow them to publish your article online. Such rights should be negotiated separately than first rights or other rights; if they aren't spelled out clearly in the contract, then ask. Similar to print rights, the electronic rights clause may involve the terms "first," "one-time" (one-time publication on the Web), or "exclusive" (the rights under contract are not available to anyone else during the terms stated). It's also important to be aware of the publication's archiving policy as it applies to online content: How long will your article be available for access online? The answer to this question—and to other electronic rights questions—will be different depending on whether the publication is an e-zine or a print publication that publishes selected articles online.

When you peruse a market guide, notice what rights magazines purchase. Most will state first rights or one-time rights, but others may demand *all* rights. When you sell all rights, you lose the right to reproduce an article unless you can negotiate for the rights to be returned to you later. *Highlights* has traditionally requested all rights from its authors because its editors like to stockpile manuscripts for the future. But Kent Brown, editor-in-chief emeritus of *Highlights* and executive director of the Highlights Foundation, has always assured his writers that he is happy to negotiate a return of rights to authors if they ask. So know what you are selling. It is more than just an article, it is the right to share that article with an audience.

Another clause you should be aware of states when to expect payment. Some publishers pay *on acceptance* of a manuscript, which means you receive a check when the manuscript is complete and the editor has officially accepted it for publication (this may mean after editing). Another option is payment *on publication*. Your check will arrive after your article hits the newsstands. When you are figuring out a household budget the timing of a payment may make a big difference as to whether you buy that new couch now or in six months.

Selling a Nonfiction Book

Just like the magazine market, the book industry has a variety of payment options and copyright clauses. Your job is to read the market guides so you can make the best choice for you as well as for the placement of your manuscript.

An author may be paid a percentage of the book's sales, called a royalty. The percentage may range from 2% to 10% or more and may be based on the book's retail price or the net price, which is the actual price received by the publishing company. Royalties may be fixed, or based on a sliding scale that depends on how many copies have been sold.

A publisher may offer an advance against royalties, which means you would receive a certain amount at the signing of the contract or in installments, and then earn royalties once the book has "paid out." For example, if your advance is $3,000, the book will have to earn more than $3,000 in royalties before you receive your first royalty check.

Many educational publishers, however, pay their writers a flat fee, known as a work-for-hire contract. It does not matter how many books are sold; the fee is set. Many writers earn their living writing several work-for-hire projects a year. Once you are established with the company, your pay may increase.

When you sign any book contract you are granting the publisher certain rights to your work. Work-for-hire contracts typically involve the purchase of all rights, while royalty contracts vary. The list of rights may include the right to reprint portions of the work; or make audio recordings, computer programs, film and television programs, foreign language editions, and—our favorite—electronic formats "now conceived or to be conceived." (Only attorneys would think of purchasing rights to something that has not been invented yet.) There are many good books on the subject of contracts and you can always consult a publishing attorney or an experienced writer for advice.

> When you sign any book contract you are granting the publisher certain rights to your work.

But when you look at a contract there is one common sense item that you need to check: Can you work within the time frame they have given you? The contract will state a date when the manuscript must be delivered. If there is a problem, now is the time to negotiate, before the title is slotted into a publisher's tight production schedule.

Websites for Writers

You need not feel alone when you are writing at your desk. A whole host of professionals are just a click away, ready to answer questions and provide support. Here are just a few sites you should bookmark:

American Society of Journalists and Authors, www.asja.org. This website gives professional freelance writers a forum to share information on writer's fees, contracts, markets, conferences, and writing resources.

Authors Guild, www.authorsguild.org. It offers contract advice, information regarding writers' rights, and current news surrounding legal issues that affect writers today.

Children's Book Council, www.cbcbooks.org. This organization for publishers of children's trade books offers a directory of publishers and authors/illustrators, as well as advice on getting published.

Publishers Weekly, www.publishersweekly.com. *Children's Bookshelf, PW*'s online newsletter, gives weekly updates on what's happening in the publishing world—what books are hitting it big, which editors have moved, and what companies are closing or merging.

The Purple Crayon, www.underdown.org. Created by Harold Underdown, a children's book editor and author of *The Complete Idiot's Guide to Publishing Children's Books*, this site offers lots of good advice on writing, illustrating, and publishing children's books.

WritersMarket, www.writersmarket.com. By subscribing to this site you can get up-to-date information on potential markets.

The Publishing Process

As the writer, you are only the first cog in the publishing process. The idea originated with you, but a child will not see a finished product until a fleet of other talented professionals adds to it. More eyes will scour your manuscript than you can imagine. Your primary contact person will be the editor, the best friend a writer can have.

Working with an Editor

Working with an editor is not like working for any other kind of employer. You may never meet, and you may not even talk much on the phone because email is often the preferred method of communication.

Even though this is a long-distance relationship, don't be shy. If you have a question, ask it. It is better to get any confusion straightened out early so there are no delays later on in the project. Editors are your ally in making your manuscript the best it can be. They have the advantage of reading your nonfiction story with a fresh eye. They can see its overall shape, and point out any gaps in the flow of information. They'll point out problems and offer suggestions or alternatives. They will also ask questions.

Your editor may question a fact that seems suspect for one reason or another. Perhaps you did not explain it clearly enough, or back it up with appropriate refer-

> Even though this is a long-distance relationship, don't be shy. If you have a question, ask it.

ences. Or the editor may not be familiar with the information. For example, in the book *Bugs for Lunch*, the artist painted a beautiful two-page spread showing a trout leaping out of the water to catch a fly. The editor flagged that picture with a note saying, "I don't think a fish would leave the water to eat." I answered her query explaining that trout often leap out of the water for insects and sent a couple of supporting references.

When Peggy and I wrote *New York: The Empire State*, our editor questioned the validity of the statement that "Salamanca is the only city in the United States that is owned by a Native American tribe." We dug deeper and found that Tuba City in Arizona is on reservation land also. However, further research revealed that Salamanca lies entirely within native land and that the Seneca Nation has remained in possession of the legal title, which had never been relinquished to either federal or state government. So we altered our statement to more accurately reflect the information.

For a single manuscript there may be dozens of comments and questions from the editor. Take your time and respond thoughtfully. Some queries may not change the manuscript at all. Others may result in a slight alteration in the wording of a sentence, or require additional research and major revision. The point is twofold: Check your facts, and be glad that editors worry about the little things.

> Even though the only person you will probably have contact with is your editor, many other people will have their hand in getting your manuscript into published form.

Besides questions on post-it notes or scribbled in the margin, your editor will also line edit your manuscript. The first time you see it, all the chicken scratches tracked across each page may awe you. These are standard proofreader's marks. Become familiar with them. All editors use them and you should too. You can find a complete list of editorial marks in *The Chicago Manual of Style*. However, you might not even have a hard copy to edit. Your editor may ask you to submit your manuscript electronically via email. In this case, your editor's comments and corrections will be made online.

Teamwork

Even though the only person you will probably have contact with is your editor, many other people will have their hand in getting your manuscript into published form. The editor will be the first to edit your manuscript for style and content. Then a copy editor will review your manuscript. A good copy editor is a treasure. His or her job is to edit for correct punctuation, grammar, capitalization, and consistency, and mark design elements such as headers and titles to make sure they conform to the publisher's house style. For example, if the publisher requires all its authors to use the third person pronoun, the copy editor will check to be sure that your manuscript complies.

You may think you turned in a nearly perfect manuscript, but that's hardly ever the case. The copy editor will fix tiny flaws that affect readability, ultimately improving your prose. For example, the previous sentence was edited from "She will fix all those tiny flaws that will improve your prose" so that we didn't misleadingly imply that flaws improved prose.

A fact checker also reviews your manuscript, verifying each piece of information with the sources that you have provided as well as others. He or she might work freelance, or as an intern at the publishing house or magazine. Sometimes the fact checker is an expert who specializes in the book's subject matter. If the fact checker finds a fact that is wrong or questionable, he or she will make a notation and provide three corroborating sources. Such a find can feel devastating to a nonfiction writer because one error can cast suspicion on your integrity and the veracity of your research process. Double check your facts and answer all queries. An error may be fixed simply by clarifying

> A fact checker also reviews your manuscript, verifying each piece of information with the sources that you have provided as well as others.

why you cited one date rather than another, or why you value one source over another. Be thankful for the opportunity to make your manuscript as accurate as possible before your readers see it.

Your book or article is not text alone, so it needs the artistic eye of an art director who is responsible for the overall design of each page—the placement of photographs or illustrations; the size, style, and color of the typeface; and the size of margins. You will not have input into these decisions.

If you are required to supply photographs, find out what format the publisher prefers. A computer JPEG file or camera-ready prints? And if the project is being illustrated, you might be asked to provide reference material for the illustrator. You have already done the research and are probably familiar with where to find such material.

For a magazine piece, you may not see the artwork until that particular issue arrives in your mailbox. Some book editors may ask you to check sketches for accuracy, but most of the time you will not see the illustrations until they send you page proofs, which show the text and art as it will appear in the book. Trust your editor and art director to pair your manuscript with the right illustrator. It may not be what you had in mind. It is usually better. The page proofs are then read by—you guessed it—a proofreader, who will make sure that all corrections have been implemented and check for last-minute mistakes.

It is not unusual for an editor to have your manuscript for months, and then return it asking for your revisions by the following week.

The production of a magazine is faster paced than the book business, but your article will undergo as thorough a treatment as a book manuscript. When your article was purchased it was slated for a particular issue six months or more in the future, so these editors work quickly fitting it into the magazine's format. Books, on the other hand, may be printed overseas, which is often less expensive than printing in the United States. Your editor keeps the book on schedule as it marches toward a specific fall or spring release date a year or two away.

It is not unusual for an editor to have your manuscript for months, and then return it asking for your revisions by the following week. Do your best to adhere to deadlines. But if there is a conflict and you need more time, call your editor and tell her. If you are flexible and amiable to work with, your editor will be more likely to give you additional time when you need it.

Months after you last saw the page proofs and while you are deep in research for another project, a box will arrive on your front porch. Once you realize what it contains, you will scoop it up, rip it open, and—for the first time—see your book in finished form. Relish the moment. It is the sweet culmination of months or years of work.

The Courage to Tell the Truth

The emotions that come with having a book published are similar to those of raising a child. This work that was with you for so long, stewing in the idea stage, being written and revised again and again, suddenly has its own identity, a life. It will find its way into the hands of kids you may never meet, and help you connect with people across the country. Your heart will flutter with fond recognition each time you see it on a library shelf, in a store window, or in the pages of a catalog. You'll want to nudge the person next to you just as you did at your child's track meets and say with pride, "That one's mine."

But another idea is already brewing. Another article is in the mail and another proposal glows beneath the cursor on your computer screen. The life of a nonfiction writer is a constant procession of job interviews in the form of query letters and proposals. And we all struggle to find enough time to devote to our craft. It is the number one complaint. But we can take the advice of scientist Santiago Ramón y Cajal who said: "If our professions do not allow us to devote more than two hours a day to a subject, do not abandon the work on the pretext that we need four hours or six. A little each day is enough as long as a little is produced each day." Underline that: *A little each day is enough as long as a little is produced each day.* The point is you are just as much a writer if you write two hours a day as someone who writes for eight. The key is that you *write*. The publishing business is not a race of the swift. It is a pursuit for the persistent.

Writing nonfiction is an internal challenge to get your facts right, to craft the proper form, and to tell the story as best you can. We have always enjoyed this challenge and, in the process of creating these creatures of truth, we have learned a lot about ourselves.

If you have ever stood before a child who has just asked where babies come from, or what happened to Rover, you know the courage it takes to tell them the truth. It takes the same bravery to write children's nonfiction.

Be bold, and we hope you, too, enjoy telling true stories to children.

Before We Say Goodbye

One of the perks of being a children's author is being invited into classrooms to talk about your writing and to share your experiences. It is a great way to promote sales, create valuable name recognition among teachers and librarians, and even get ideas. The best part is seeing firsthand how your book touches a child's life.

No matter what grade level you address, be prepared to answer questions. How old are you? When did you start writing? What is your favorite book? Do you have a dog? Have you met J. K. Rowling? Children want to know everything. And a child will eventually ask you why you became a nonfiction writer. What will you tell them? Who encouraged you? What events transpired to set you in search of true stories?

There will be times when you feel like a star as you walk under hand-painted banners proclaiming your arrival. Other moments will be more humbling. Once when I announced that I had time for one last question, a little girl raised her hand and asked, "Can we go now?"

You may be wondering the same thing. I guess we've said enough. Yes, you can go now.

Margery Facklam and Peggy Thomas

Children's Books That Inspired Us

We suggest that you explore these books as you develop your own nonfiction projects.

Adler, David. *A Hero and the Holocaust: The Story of Janusz Korzcak and His Children*

Arnold, Caroline. *A Panda's World*
    Giant Sea Reptiles of the Dinosaur Age
    When Mammoths Walked the Earth

Arnosky, Jim. *The Brook Book: Exploring the Smallest Streams*
    Secrets of a Wildlife Watcher

Aronson, Marc. *Sir Walter Ralegh and the Quest for El Dorado*

Barretta, Gene. *Now & Ben: The Modern Inventions of Benjamin Franklin*

Bartoletti, Susan Campbell. *Growing Up in Coal Country*
    Hitler Youth: Growing Up in Hitler's Shadow

Barton, Chris. *The Day-Glo Brothers: The True Story of Bob and Joe Switzer's Bright Ideas and Brand-New Colors*

Bausum, Ann. *Freedom Riders: John Lewis and Jim Zwerg on the Front Lines of the Civil Rights Movement*

Bayrock, Fiona. *Bubble Homes and Fish Farts*

Berne, Jennifer. *Manfish: A Story of Jacques Cousteau*

Bortz, Fred. *Astrobiology*

Butterworth, Chris. *Sea Horse: The Shyest Fish in the Sea*

Butts, Nancy. *Nature's Numbers*

Carlson, Laurie. *Thomas Edison for Kids: His Life and Ideas, 21 Activities*

Chadwick, Roxane. *Amelia Earhart: Aviation Pioneer*

Cummins, Julie and Cheryl Harness. *Women Daredevils: Thrills, Chills, and Frills*

Curlee, Lynn. *Brooklyn Bridge*

Davies, Nicola. *Just the Right Size: Why Big Animals Are Big and Little Animals Are Little*

Dokken, Kay. *Will a Clownfish Make You Giggle? Answers to Some Very Fishy Questions*

Editors of *TIME For Kids* with Kathryn Hoffman Satterfield. *TIME For Kids: Benjamin Franklin: A Man of Many Talents*

Ellyard, David. *Whose Idea Was That? Inventions That Changed Our Lives*

Feldman, Eve. *Benjamin Franklin: Scientist and Inventor*

Additional Resources

Fleischman, Sid. *Sir Charlie: Chaplin, The Funniest Man in the World*
  The Trouble Begins at 8: A Life of Mark Twain in the Wild, Wild West

Fleming, Candace. *Ben Franklin's Almanac: Being a True Account of the Good
  Gentleman's Life*
    *The Great and Only Barnum: The Tremendous, Stupendous Life of Showman P. T.
      Barnum*

Fox, Karen C. *Older Than the Stars*

Fradin, Dennis Brindell. *Who Was Ben Franklin?*

Freedman, Russell. *Lincoln: A Photobiography*
    Immigrant Kids

Fritz, Jean. *Leonardo's Horse*

George, Jean Craighead. *The First Thanksgiving*
    The Moon of the Deer

Gibbons, Gail. *Dinosaurs*

Giblin, James Cross. *Chimney Sweeps: Yesterday and Today*
    Charles A. Lindbergh: A Human Hero
    *From Hand to Mouth: Or, How We Invented Knives, Forks, Spoons, and Chopsticks
      and the Table Manners To Go With Them*
    Good Brother, Bad Brother: The Story of Edwin Booth and John Wilkes Booth
    The Life and Death of Adolf Hitler
    Thomas Jefferson: A Picture Book Biography

Goodman, Susan E. *Claws, Coats and Camouflage: The Ways Animals Fit Into Their
  World*

Graves, Charles Parlin. *Benjamin Franklin: Man of Ideas*

Harness, Cheryl. *Abe Lincoln Goes to Washington*

Heiligman, Deborah. *Charles and Emma: The Darwins' Leap of Faith*

Holyoke, Nancy. *HELP! A Girl's Guide to Divorce and Stepfamilies*

Hoose, Phillip. *Claudette Colvin: Twice Toward Justice*
    The Race to Save the Lord God Bird

Johmann, Carol. *The Lewis and Clark Expedition*

Kramer, Barbara. *John Glenn: A Space Biography*

Krull, Kathleen. *Houdini: World's Greatest Mystery Man and Escape King*
    Lincoln Tells a Joke: How Laughter Saved the President (and the Country)

Kudlinski, Kathleen. *Boy, Were We Wrong About Dinosaurs*

Lauber, Patricia. *Hurricanes*

Macaulay, David. *The Way Things Work*

Mattern, Joanne. *The Big Book of the Civil War: Fascinating Facts about the Civil War, Including Historic Photographs, Maps, and Documents*

McMillan, Bruce. *Summer Ice: Life Along the Antarctic Peninsula*

McNulty, Faith. *If You Decide To Go To the Moon*

Meltzer, Milton. *Voices from the Civil War*

Miller, Brandon Marie. *George Washington for Kids: His Life and Times*

Montgomery, Sy. *Quest for the Tree Kangaroo: An Expedition to the Cloud Forest of New Guinea*
   Saving the Ghost of the Mountain, An Expedition Among Snow Leopards in Mongolia
   The Tarantula Scientist

Murphy, Jim. *An American Plague*
   The Boys' War: Confederate and Union Soldiers Talk About the Civil War
   The Great Fire
   A *Young Patriot: The American Revolution as Experienced by One Boy*

Myers, Walter Dean. *The Greatest: Muhammad Ali*

Nelson, Kadir. *We Are the Ship: The Story of Negro League Baseball*

Pringle, Laurence. *Crows! Strange and Wonderful*

Rau, Dana Meachen. *Alternative Energy: Beyond Fossil Fuels*

Ritchey, Kate. *Creepy Crafts for Boys and Ghouls*

Roop, Peter and Connie. *Take Command, Captain Farragut!*

Ryan, Pam Muños. *When Marian Sang*

Senisi, Ellen B. *Berry Smudges and Leaf Prints: Finding and Making Colors from Nature*

Simon, Seymour. *The Heart: Our Circulatory System*

St. George, Judith. *Make Your Mark, Franklin Roosevelt*
   So You Want to Be President?

Stone, Tanya Lee. *Almost Astronauts: 13 Women Who Dared to Dream*

Thimmesh, Catherine. *Team Moon: How 400,000 People Landed Apollo 11 on the Moon*

Tingum, Janice. *E. B. White: The Elements of a Writer*

Waldman, Neil. *They Came from the Bronx: How the Buffalo were Saved From Extinction*

Weatherford, Carole Boston. *Moses: When Harriet Tubman Led Her People to Freedom*

White, E. B. *Charlotte's Web*

Winters, Kay. *Abe Lincoln: The Boy Who Loved Books*

Yolen, Jane. *My Brothers' Flying Machine: Wilbur, Orville, and Me*

Selected Books by Margery Facklam and Peggy Thomas

Facklam, Margery. *And Then There Was One: The Mysteries of Extinction*
  Bees Dance and Whales Sing: The Mysteries of Animal Communication
  Behind These Doors: Science Museum Makers
  The Big Bug Book
  Bugs for Lunch
  Creepy, Crawly Caterpillars
  I Eat Dinner
  I Go to Sleep
  Spiders and Their Web Sites
  Tracking Dinosaurs in the Gobi
  What's the Buzz? The Secret Life of Bees
  Who Harnessed the Horse? The Story of Animal Domestication
  What Does the Crow Know? The Mysteries of Animal Intelligence
  Wild Animals, Gentle Women

Facklam, Margery and Howard. *Changes in the Wind: Earth's Shifting Climate*
  From Cell to Clone: The Story of Genetic Engineering
  Healing Drugs: The History of Pharmacology
  Spare Parts for People

Facklam, Margery and Patricia Phibbs. *Corn-Husk Crafts*

Facklam, Margery and Peggy Thomas. *The Kids' World Almanac of Amazing Facts*
  About Numbers, Math and Money
  New York: The Empire State

Thomas, Peggy. *Artificial Intelligence*
  Bird Alert
  Bacteria and Viruses
  Farmer George Plants a Nation
  For the Birds: The Life of Roger Tory Peterson
  Grace Hopper: Computer Pioneer
  Marine Mammal Preservation
  Medicines from Nature
  Post-Traumatic Stress Disorder
  Talking Bones: The Science of Forensic Anthropology
  Volcano!

Index

Index

Index